Jackie Robinson

My Own Story

As Told by Jackie Robinson to Wendell Smith
Foreword by Branch Rickey

**ALLEGRO
EDITIONS**

Published by Allegro Editions
ISBN: 978-1-62654-940-1

Printed in the U. S. A.

FOREWORD BY

BRANCH RICKEY

Jackie Robinson has asked me to write a Foreword to
his book, which is an autobiography beginning with his
athletic career and dealing particularly with baseball.
It seems to me, it must have been very difficult to tell his
story.

In writing this book, Robinson, I am sure, did not
intend to create the impression that he has already
achieved ultimate success as a player or that his advent
to   baseball represents any more than the first step
toward equal participation by Negroes in this great
American sport. I know that, above all, he intended to
make good as a ball player when he first joined the
Brooklyn organization. Nevertheless, he sensed the deli-
cate racial responsibility which his association with white
players involved.

Jackie is well educated, as we generally understand that
word. He is a good sportsman and a gentleman. On the
field he has proven himself to be a good player with fine
physical abilities and most unusual aptitudes.

His appearance with the Brooklyn Club in the spring
of 1947 was marked in a most singular manner. He had
never been a first baseman; his knowledge of the position
derived exclusively from observation. He did a grand
job as the regular first baseman, and helped materially
to win the National League pennant for the Brooklyn
Club.

His greatest achievement, however, in my judgment,
was his tactful handling of his relationship with his fellow players, as well as his opponents; and the fact that

he was able to maintain the favorable regard of the press and the public.

Jackie is naturally a competitor—a combative competitor. He resents unfairness or unsportsmanlike play directed toward his team or himself. Under no circumstances, however, could he allow himself to show resentment. Only those on the team know the great patience and self-control he exercised continuously throughout the season. For this exemplary conduct, displayed both off and on the field during the entire season, he deserves the commendation of everyone.

The book bespeaks the modesty and tact characteristic of his playing and general demeanor. I hope, in this new venture that he will have a sympathetic audience; I hope the sportswriters and fans will receive his book as readily as they have received his work on the playing field.

I believe that a man's race, color, and religion should never constitute a handicap. The denial to anyone, anywhere, any time of equality of opportunity to work is incomprehensible to me. Moreover, I believe that the American public is not as concerned with a first baseman's pigmentation as it is with the power of his swing, the dexterity of his slide, the gracefulness of his fielding, or the speed of his legs.

And finally, here's hoping that this is the first of many good books this young man may write.

Contents

Born to Play Games

I WAS BORN ON JANUARY 31, 1919, IN CAIRO, GEORGIA, a little town near the Georgia-Florida line. My family named me John Roosevelt Robinson, after Teddy Roosevelt. They tell me I must have been destined to play on a ball club managed by Leo Durocher, because I immediately started squawking as though a bad decision had been called on me. And in one sense, it had. Every child born into poverty has one or two strikes on him before he starts the game.

I was the youngest of five children. The others were Matthew, Edgar, Willa Mae, and Frank. My father died a year after I was born, and my mother, Mollie Robinson, became the sole support for a family of five. By superhuman effort she carried on, toiling endless hours at all sorts of heavy manual labor. Those were hard times for all of us, but particularly for her. Yet, wonderful woman that she is, she was not content merely to feed and clothe us. She was determined to see that we got an education and had a chance to amount to something. Realizing that southern Georgia was hardly a land of opportunity for poor Negroes, she somehow mustered the means and the courage to move us to Pasadena, California, to live. It was still a constant struggle to make ends meet, but we kids began to help out by doing odd jobs, and at the same time we were going to school—to good schools. That was what Mother had set her heart on.

As soon as I was old enough, I contributed my bit by shining shoes, running errands, selling newspapers, and hawking hot dogs at the baseball parks and football stadiums. Yet I had time for play, too, like any average kid. My cousins and I used to shag flies for older boys, and I can remember discovering then that I could run faster than most of the kids in our neighborhood.

Athletics, both school and professional, come nearer to offering an American Negro equality of opportunity than does any other field of social and economic activity. Fortunately, both my brother Matthew — "Mack," we called him — and I had some athletic ability. It made the going much easier for us than for our Negro schoolmates who were not athletically inclined.

Mack was a great athlete. He became famous long before anyone ever heard of me. He established the junior college broad jump record with a leap of twenty-five feet, and at the University of Oregon he became literally a one-man track team. He set a world record of 20.7 seconds for the 220 yard dash — a record that stood until Jesse Owens broke it a few years later. These feats won him a place in our 1936 Olympic team.

Naturally, Mack was my idol. I used to watch him perform and say to myself: "Gee, I'd like to be a great athlete some day! I'd like to be like Mack."

My first athletic achievements were as a softball player. I went in for all the other sports, too, but I liked softball the best. At Muir Technical High School in Pasadena, I played football and basketball, ran on the track team, but took only a mild interest in baseball.

When I finished high school, I entered Pasadena Junior College and rapidly developed into a pretty good all-around athlete. My proudest achievement, I think, was breaking Mack's broad jump record. I leaped twenty-five feet, six and one-third inches—as against his twenty-five feet. To eclipse one's idol, even in one event, is a great thrill to any boy.

Since UCLA was nearby, I decided I would enroll there. Football, of course, was the major college sport. I loved to play it, and I was considered a good college prospect. One incident revealed to me the almost absurd emphasis on the game. When it became known that I was going to do my college work at UCLA, a devoted Stanford alumnus came to me and offered to finance my way through any school in the East that was not on Stanford's football schedule. He didn't want me to play against his Stanford teams!

Strange as it may seem now, I made a better record at UCLA in football, basketball, and track than I did in baseball. I guess I didn't put as much effort into baseball as I did into the other sports. Like most Negro athletes, I just assumed that baseball was a sport without a professional future. I played it solely for the fun of it. Football, on the other hand, held out some kind of a future. Professional teams in the Pacific Coast Leagues did not discriminate against Negro players. The same was true of basketball. There were any number of professional teams made up of both whites and Negroes.

Those were happy days at UCLA. I was a college star, a campus hero — the height of most American boys' ambition. In 1938 I was the leading ground-gainer of the United States, with an average of twelve yards everytime I carried the ball. In basketball, I led the Pacific Coast Conference in scoring, with 148 points. And before I left school I was named on a number of All-American teams. I was also a member of the Pacific Coast track team that defeated the Big Ten team in a meet at Northwestern. I broke the conference record in the broadjump, and later on won that event in the N.C.A.A. meet at Minneapolis.

It seemed I could never get enough of games and

9

sports. When I wasn't engaged in college competition, I played shortstop on the Pasadena baseball team that won the state amateur title. I'm afraid the quality of our play was not very high, because I compiled a batting average of .400, and in one game I remember stealing seven bases! When I could find the time, I'd go out to the golf course; but the best I could shoot was in the middle eighties. I also took a crack at tennis and reached the quarter finals in the Southern California Negro tournament. I even learned to play a fair game of table-tennis!

My mother wanted me to concentrate on my studies. She wanted me to become a doctor, or a lawyer, or a coach. I wasn't interested in the first two, but I did like the coaching idea. It gave me an excuse to play games all the time. "If I'm going to be a coach," I'd tell her, "I'll have to keep playing. You can't teach a game if you don't know it."

After the war, I did do some coaching at a small Negro college in Texas. I enjoyed it and they seemed to be satisfied with me.

In 1942 I joined the United States Army and was commissioned a year later. I was discharged in November, 1944, and the following spring I joined the Kansas City Monarchs as a shortstop.

There have not been many romances in my life. I liked Rachel Isum the first time I met her, and we went together throughout our college years. She was an honor student, majoring in nursing. We got engaged, but she almost broke it when I joined the Kansas City team. She didn't want me traveling all over the country with a barnstorming team. "We'll never be together," she said. "How can we ever learn enough about each other to get married?"

I assured her that I wouldn't stay in baseball long. "All I want to do," I told her, "is to make some money. They're going to pay me a hundred dollars a week. I've got to help my mother out and I don't know anywhere I can make that much money right away."

Rachel understood, but she didn't like it. She wanted me to get a job in Los Angeles.

So I went with Kansas City only because I needed the money. I never dreamed of becoming a full-time professional baseball player. All the time I was playing, I was looking around for something else. I didn't like the bouncing buses, the cheap hotels, and the constant night games.

But I did meet some great ball players that year. Two of them — Satchel Paige and Josh Gibson — would have starred in any league that ever was. Modern baseball has produced few pitchers the equal of Paige and few hitters that could match Gibson. If those two had only been given the chance I was to have, their names would have been somewhere near the top in the record books. But it's too late now. Satch is no longer young, and Josh is dead.

I saw Paige in action many times. He was pitching for the Monarchs that season. I remember thinking to myself what a wizard he must have been in his prime — he could still do anything he wanted to with a baseball! It seems actually tragic to me that Paige never got to pitch in a Major League game.

I remember one of our games in Cleveland. Satchel was pitching and the game went into the ninth, a scoreless tie. As Satchel walked past our opponents' bench, he said "You fellows better run down to the hotel and get some sandwiches. It's almost supper time."

They wanted to know what sandwiches had to do with it.

"Well," Satch' said, "if we don't score, you sure in hell ain't. Why, we're likely to be here until tomorrow this time."

11

And, they didn't score, either! We finally won it about four innings later.

After I joined the Monarchs, Rachel went to New York to do graduate work. I kept playing ball and wondering if I was going to lose my girl. Then came my lucky break. The Dodgers signed me to play with Montreal, and Rachel and I knew then that we could be together because I'd be with a team that played as much at home as it did away.

Mr. Rickey apparently believes a ball player is better off married. When I signed the contract to play with Montreal, he asked me if I had a girl I'd like to marry. "Yes, sir," I said, "I have a girl friend."

"Well," he ordered, "you marry her right away!"

He said it just like that. It probably didn't even occur to him that Rachel had something to say about that. I was supposed to go play winter ball in Venezuela with my friend Roy Campanella, who later played with Montreal. Rachel and I decided to get married before I left. But after talking it over carefully, we thought it would be best to wait until I returned in January.

When I returned from South America, we got married.

My wife has meant everything to me. She has inspired me all the time, pushing me on, encouraging me when things looked black, and always assuring me that I could do anything any other ball player could. I do not believe I could have made the grade without her help.

When my wife gave birth to a bouncing baby boy, we named him Jackie, Jr. and vowed that we'd give him all the things we had missed as kids.

My athletic career has been a full one, and I have enjoyed almost all of it. I hope my son will be an athlete, too. I am sure it will keep him out of trouble. A lot of boys get in trouble because they don't have anything to do. When they're playing games, wrestling, or boxing, they don't have time to loaf on street corners or get mixed up with tough gangs. Sports have kept me out of plenty trouble.

A coach once told me that a gymnasium often makes the difference between a criminal and a good citizen. I agree with him. I only wish we had more gymnasiums in this country for our kids, and I'm sure that they do, too.

My Lucky Star

IT WAS LATE IN AUGUST OF 1945 AND I WAS COMPLET-
ing my first year in professional baseball with the
Kansas City Monarchs. We were playing the Chicago
American Giants at Comiskey Park in Chicago, and just
before the game got under way, a man leaned over the
rail near our dugout and introduced himself to me.

"I'm Clyde Sukeforth," he said almost apologetically.
"I represent the Brooklyn Dodgers's organization. I came
out here today to see you play."

I shook his hand and said I was glad to meet him.
Actually, I was neither impressed nor elated. Down
through the years an athlete meets a lot of people. Some
of them are exactly who they say they are, but there are
others who assume names and titles just as a matter of
convenience.

When I was playing football at UCLA, people were
always coming around and introducing· themselves as
celebrities. Some of them really were, but a lot of times
I found out they were harmless imposters. It is amusing
to what lengths some people will go to get close to an
athlete.

One time, for instance, we were running out on the field
at UCLA for a big game. Just before we came out from
under the stands a fellow stepped in front of me, grabbed
my hand, and said, "I'm Mr. So-and-so." It upset me for
a moment because all I had on my mind was the game.

14

He made a great long speech on the chances of our winning the game. He was a rather distinguished-looking man and said he was the secretary to some one whose name I recognized as that of a Los Angeles millionaire.

Some time later I actually did meet this millionaire and during the course of the conversation I told him that I had met his secretary. I recalled the name. The man laughed and said, "My secretary? Why that fellow's the janitor in the building where I live." Similar incidents had happened to me before. I made up my mind right then and there that in the future I would be skeptical of people who dropped down out of nowhere and introduced themselves to me.

Consequently, when Clyde Sukeforth said he represented the Brooklyn Dodgers and had come to the game specifically to see me play, I almost laughed in his pleasant, clean-cut face. I was sure that this fellow standing before me was just another crackpot.

Sukeforth here to scout me for the Brooklyn Dodgers of the National League? No one could tell me that. As far as I was concerned, neither the Dodgers nor any other Major League team, was thinking of signing a Negro player, any more than of signing a member of a girls' soft-ball team.

In April of that same year, I had gone to Boston under the auspices of the *Pittsburgh Courier* for a tryout with the Red Sox. Two other Negro players were with me: Sammy Jethroe, an outfielder of the Cleveland Buckeyes, and Marvin Williams, a second baseman of the Philadelphia Stars. We went to Fenway Park and worked out with a group of sandlot kids. Joe Cronin, then Manager of the Red Sox, and Mr. Collins watched us perform. After the workout they shook hands with us and told us we might hear from them. We never did.

When I left Sukeforth and sat down in the dugout with the rest of the Kansas City players, one of them

15

asked, "Who's the white fellow you were talking with, Jackie?"

"I don't know," I said. "He says he's scouting me for the Brooklyn Dodgers."

Everyone on the bench laughed, including me. One of the players jumped up and saluted me. "I'm a scout, too," he said, standing very erect. "I'm from Moose Face Troop No. 60 and if I pass my Eagle test next week, I'm gonna' fly away."

We all got a great kick out of it. The possibility of a Big League scout spending his time looking at Negro players was nothing but a joke. Everyone agreed, and by the time the game started I had practically forgotten Sukeforth.

But when it was over and I came out of the dressing room, he was standing there. I nodded and started to walk past him. I didn't want to be bothered with this screw-ball. I wanted to get to the Grand Hotel on the South Side and get my dinner. I was hungry as the devil. But Sukey — as I came to call him later — stopped me. I wanted to tell him to leave me alone. But he was so courteous and soft-spoken that I just couldn't.

As we walked along the street, he talked to me. "Mr. Rickey wants me to bring you to Brooklyn," he said. "He wants to have a talk with you."

"When?" I asked, almost disdainfully.

"He wants to see you tomorrow, if possible," Sukeforth said. "He's really anxious to talk with you."

I don't know whether I looked like a growling dog or not, but Sukeforth must have heard the annoyance in my voice when I said, "Come on now, stop kidding. What the devil do you want? I'm hungry. I want to go eat."

Sukeforth shook his head as though he considered me a hopeless case. But he didn't give up. "I'm telling you the truth," he said. "Now you get yourself together and come on like you have some sense in that head of yours."

His commanding voice was not insulting. I stopped walking suddenly and looked at him. "You mean that you're taking me to Brooklyn yourself to see Mr. Rickey?" I asked.

"Yes," he said. "He wants to see you and I'm acting under instructions to take you to him right away."

By now it was almost dark. The moon was peeking over lazy clouds that seemed to be hanging in the evening dusk. Trying to think clearly, I looked up and saw a great shining star in the northern skies. It was so bright I couldn't take my eyes off it.

It's peculiar the things men will think about when their whole future may be at stake. You read stories about men in battle, surrounded by the enemy and with death staring them in the face, who are thinking about the folks back home, wondering what shift Dad is working — afternoon or night. Or if Danville's still in first place in the Three-I League. . . .

I was in some such mental state when Sukey said he was going to take me to Brooklyn.

My subconscious mind seemed to be blotting out my conscious thoughts. "Why don't you pay attention to what this man is saying?" I told myself. "You must be going crazy. Here's a man standing before you, offering you a chance to go to Brooklyn and talk with the owner of the Dodgers. You might even get a chance to play with them someday."

Sukeforth was standing there looking at me, waiting for an answer. He was ready to take me on the most important journey I had ever taken. He was ready to take me to a man who could shape my whole destiny, who could grant me an opportunity in a field never before open to my people.

"Maybe," I said to myself, "that star is especially bright tonight for you. Maybe Someone is trying to lead you.

Maybe He is up there trying to tell you to go see Mr. Rickey."

"Listen," I said to Sukeforth as I came out of my coma, "I am making one hundred dollars each and every week with the Kansas City Monarchs. If I go to Brooklyn tonight and don't show up here for tomorrow's game, I'll get fired."

Sukeforth smiled. "Don't worry about that," he said, giving me an assuring slap on the back. "I think you've seen your last days with Kansas City."

I didn't know what to do. We started walking again, Sukeforth strolling along beside me. I wanted to go some place and sit down and think, but I couldn't tell him to leave me alone. He was being too nice and too patient.

Suddenly I became disgusted with myself. Why the reluctance? Why the hesitancy? After all, it was a gamble; you don't get any place in life if you don't take a risk once in awhile. If I did go to Brooklyn and this all turned out to be a hoax, I could probably get a job with some other team. Maybe Kansas City wouldn't fire me. Maybe Mr. Wilkerson, the owner of the team, would overlook it and forget all about it.

I knew that if I did go to Brooklyn it wouldn't take me long to find out what was going on. I knew that after I had talked with Mr. Rickey ten minutes, I'd know what the future held in store for me. Kansas City, I reasoned, couldn't find a new shortstop that quickly.

Sukeforth interrupted my thoughts. "You'd better hurry and make up your mind," he said kindly. "We don't have too much time."

He was right. I'd have to pack, eat, and get to the station in less than an hour. "Okay," I said, "I'll go. I don't know if I'm doing the right thing, but it's worth a gamble."

We went to my hotel and I started throwing my things in a suitcase. All the time I was saying to myself: "You better know what the devil you're doing. If you go to Brooklyn and this thing turns out to be a flop, you'll be the laughing stock of baseball. People will remember you as the guy who was dumb enough to believe that a Negro might get a chance in organized baseball. If it fails to work out, Mr. Wilkerson or Frank Duncan, the Kansas City manager, might decide they don't want a guy that dumb on their ball club."

So I decided I wouldn't tell anyone I was going. I wouldn't even tell my best friend on the team. I'd just disappear. Then, if it didn't work out, I could come back and say I just didn't feel like playing for a few days and took a little trip for a rest. No one would laugh at me for that. Some ball players do that. If they are good players and needed by the team, the manager usually forgives them, consoling himself with the theory that a good unpredictable player is better to have around than one whose only asset to the club is his habit of being on time every day.

When we got to the station, we only had about ten minutes. Sukeforth went to the window to purchase the tickets. I followed him.

"Two tickets to New York," he said to the man behind the counter. "Can you give us a bedroom?"

The ticket seller checked his chart, then suddenly looked up. "A bedroom?" he asked with a puzzled look on his face.

"Yes," Sukeforth said, "there are two of us." He pointed to me.

The ticket seller looked at Sukeforth, then at me. "He's going with you?" he asked as if to make sure Sukeforth knew what he was doing. "Sure," Sukey answered, "he's going with me. Anything wrong with that?"

"Oh no," the agent said quickly, his face reddening slightly. "I just didn't hear you at first."

He put two tickets in an envelope and handed them

19

to Sukeforth. It had never occurred to Sukeforth that the ticket agent would be surprised over our traveling together. After all, he was white and I a Negro.

Just before we boarded the train, I took one quick look back over my shoulder and up at the sky. There it was, still sparkling, and it seemed to be focused directly on me. For some silly reason, I was glad.

*B*ranch Rickey

THE FIRST TIME I MET MR. RICKEY, I REALIZED HE WAS more than just the owner of a Major League baseball club. After listening to him talk for five minutes, I was completely fascinated. He talks with such ease and grace that you find yourself listening the way a little boy pays attention to stories about Santa Claus.

When I walked into his office that bright August morning, Mr. Rickey was sitting behind his big desk. He smiled broadly and his deep-set eyes sparkled under his bushy eyebrows. "Come in, come in," he said hospitably. "I'm very glad to see you. Clyde Sukeforth tells me you're quite a ball player, Jackie."

I guess I was a little awkward. I didn't want to appear too modest, and yet I didn't want to convey the impression that I had a big head. Sukeforth, standing beside me, rose to the occasion.

"He's the Brooklyn type of player," Sukey said in that soft, accurate voice of his. "The boy can run like blazes and looks like he might be a pretty fair country hitter."

Mr. Rickey nodded approvingly. He picked up a tattered stub that had once been a reasonable facsimile of a cigar. He looked at me like a pawn broker examining some trinket brought in by an unfamiliar customer. His piercing eyes roamed over me with such meticulous care, I felt almost naked.

It was a little embarrassing. I shifted uneasily and for

21

want of something to do jammed my hand down in my coat pocket. I don't know what I expected to find there, but I guess I was searching for something to hold on to. Perhaps I'd find a pencil, or maybe some coins. I felt I needed something in my hands right then, something firm and strong.

"Do you drink?" Mr. Rickey suddenly asked.

"No, sir," I said rather proudly.

"That's fine," he said, relaxing in his chair. "Sit down, sit down. We have a lot to talk about." Sukey and I reacted to the order as though it had been given by a five-star general.

"Do you know why you are here, Jackie?" he asked.

I said all I knew was that Sukeforth had told me he had instructions to bring me to Brooklyn.

"Well," Mr. Rickey said slowly and carefully, "I am interested in bringing you into the Brooklyn organization. I have never seen you play, but my scouts have. If Sukeforth says you're a good ball player, I'll take his word for it. He's been around and knows a prospect when he sees one. He thinks, as do some of my other men, you could make good on one of our top farm clubs."

Needless to say, I was excited. The thought of playing on a farm club of a Major League team sent little electric shocks up and down my spine. Here was my chance — the chance to be affiliated with a Big League team. Even if I weren't good enough, I could someday tell my grandchildren that I had at least had the opportunity.

Then Mr. Rickey told me I would have to stand a lot of gaff without losing my temper or making a scene. He even acted out several situations I'd be likely to face, and then asked how I would meet each one of them. I wasn't too happy over the prospect he foresaw, but I knew too, that

I was pretty sure to run into some name-calling, some insults, some Jim Crow.

I told him I felt pretty sure I would stay out of rhubarbs on the field and trouble of any sort away from it, but that I couldn't become an obsequious, cringing fellow. Among other things, I couldn't play hard, aggressive ball if I were that sort of man.

Mr. Rickey seemed satisfied because he changed the subject:

"I haven't made up my mind which farm club we'll put you on," Mr. Rickey continued, "but wherever it is, I want you to understand one thing: there will be no limitations as to how far you can go. We will not consider you in any way different from the rest of the players we have in this organization. You are simply another ball player trying to make the grade. If you are good enough, you'll wind up on top. If you aren't, you'll be sent down to another league or released outright."

You could have knocked me over with a feather! Had my ears betrayed me? Could I be wide awake and of sound mind? Yes, as he continued to talk, I realized that he was serious and that I was not dreaming.

During the train ride, Sukey had told me a lot about Branch Rickey. You could see he was proud to work for such a man. He spoke of Mr. Rickey with deep respect, almost reverently. He told me of his long and courageous rise to baseball heights, conquering one adversity after another. "He isn't afraid of anything or anybody," Sukeforth boasted of his employer. "If he wants to do something — like hire you, for instance — nothing is going to stop him. He isn't stubborn, either. He just seems to know what he's doing and how to do it."

Although I had known him but a few hours, I had come to like Sukeforth and he in turn made me like Mr. Rickey before I had ever met the man. I was glad to hear Sukeforth say Branch Rickey had the courage of his convictions. Above all, that made me feel good.

During the initial meeting with him, I found Suke-forth had told me the truth. Mr. Rickey was entertaining and convincing, an excellent conversationalist. His voice is powerful and penetrating, yet neither rasping nor harsh. He can, if he wishes, thrash you or soothe you with his tongue; and he has the unusual faculty of making you think you can do the impossible.

I learned, alas, that he is a man of surprising para-doxes. As most people know, he does not attend ball games on Sunday, swear, or drink; but he does not ob-ject to other people's doing those things. "If a man chooses to swear to express himself," he once told me, "that is all right with me. I just don't do it because I consider profanity a poor and unimaginative way to con-vey your observations and impressions."

Once my interest in Mr. Rickey was aroused, I was eager to know more about him. Many of the facts of his life I learned from Mr. Rickey himself, others I picked up elsewhere. Taken together, they tell an unusual story:

Branch Rickey was born on a farm near Lucasville, Ohio, on December 20, 1881. When he finished ele-mentary school, his father decided he had had enough education and should go out and help support their large family. As a result, the boy gave up his formal education and started working, but he did not stop study-ing.

It wasn't long before he was ready to go to college. He entered Ohio Wesleyan University and worked at all sorts of jobs to earn his way through school. Besides doing manual work, he played football and baseball. When money was scarce, he went out and played these sports professionally. He never concerned himself over the virtues of amateurism—a fact that might be shock-ing to Avery Brundage, president of the Amateur Ath-letic Union.

24

In due time, Rickey received his diploma and became a teacher at Allegheny College and later at Delaware College. He continued to play semi-pro baseball and football, receiving as much as 150 dollars for playing in one football game. That was not to last long, however. In one of those bruising clashes, he was carried off the field with a broken leg. That ended his football days.

From then on, Rickey's athletic career was limited to baseball. In 1903, at the age of twenty-one, he got a trial as a catcher with the Lamar (Wyoming) Club. The next spring he opened with Dallas in the Texas League. Dallas sold him to the Cincinnati Reds and the papers stamped him as an excellent prospect. . . . But Branch Rickey had principles.

"The manager of the Cincinnati Reds, Joe Kelly, did not like it when I refused to play ball on Sunday," Mr. Rickey explained. "I was promptly sent to the St. Louis Browns."

Rickey's determination not to play on the Sabbath presented real difficulties. He went from St. Louis to the White Sox and finally to the Highlanders, who later became the New York Yankees.

In 1908 he suffered a decline in health and decided to quit baseball and go back to school. He entered the Law School of the University of Michigan. Exhibiting his customary zeal for learning, he swept through the three-year law course in two, coached the baseball team, and discovered one of baseball's all-time greats, George Sisler, whom he later took to the St. Louis Browns.

In 1911 he tacked his shingle on the door of a humble office in Boise, Idaho. The following two years were far from profitable. Clients were few and far between. This was discouraging because by now he was married and had another mouth to feed. So when Robert Hedges, owner of the St. Louis Browns, offered the young lawyer a "front office job," he immediately accepted and went to St. Louis, taking young George Sisler with him. Rickey's progressive ideas and organizational ability attracted the attention of Phil Ball, a millionaire who was interested in baseball. In 1916 Ball purchased the Browns and offered Rickey the job of general manager. He declined, however, and joined the St. Louis Cardinals' staff.

It was Rickey who conceived and shaped the Cards' famed "chain system." For a while he managed the team, but he made no bid for immortality in that capacity. He knew baseball, but his players couldn't grasp his ideas. Finally he gave up the job and moved upstairs as general manager. Almost immediately his "farms" began to produce, and before long the St. Louis Cardinals became one of the great baseball organizations.

Rickey stayed with the Cardinals for thirty years, and then in 1942 he decided he had had enough of St. Louis. He had made such a reputation as a baseball executive, however, that he wasn't out of a job long. Presently the owners of the Brooklyn Dodgers offered him the presidency of the club. He accepted and later purchased the controlling stock. Now he had a ball club of his own. He could run it according to his own dictates and desires. Just as he had done in St. Louis, he started out building up a strong farm system, And almost immediately Brooklyn's baseball fortunes began to soar, and everyone in Flatbush was happy.

Rickey had his first experience with discrimination when he was coaching baseball at Michigan. Red Smith tells the story this way. "Rickey had a Negro named Charley Thomas on the squad. The first trip the boy made was to South Bend, Ind., where the hotel management declined to let him register. Rickey blamed himself later for not having had the foresight to brief the kid in advance, preparing him for such experiences.

"Rickey and the team captain were sharing a suite. When Branch learned of Thomas's difficulties, he hurried down and asked whether the management would let Thomas move into the suite. This was agreed, provided Thomas didn't register, and all three retired to their quarters.

"Upstairs, Rickey and the captain got to talking. Thomas sat on the edge of Rickey's bed with his head low, so that his face was concealed. When Branch tried to draw him into the conversation, the boy lifted his head. He was crying. He was wringing his hands between his knees, twisting the fingers as though trying to pull the skin off.

" 'It's these,' the kid said, lifting his hands.

Rickey didn't understand.

" 'They're black,' the kid said.

" 'It's my skin,' the kid said, 'If it weren't for my skin, I wouldn't be any different from anybody.'

" 'My hands,' the kid said. 'They're black. If they were only white!'

"Rickey said, 'Tommy, the day will come when they won't have to be white.' "

When I heard about that incident, I gathered new hope. If forty-five years ago Mr. Rickey believed that a man deserved fair treatment regardless of his race or color, there was no reason to believe he had changed.

The more I learned about Branch Rickey, the more pleased I was that I was playing ball for him, was a part of his organization; and I wanted to show him I was capable of handling any situation into which he might drop me. I had never known a man like him before. Like Sukeforth, I found myself admiring him, glad to be around him, and ready to do whatever he wanted me to do.

Maybe I'm Doing Something for My Race

WHEN THE BROOKLYN DODGERS' MANAGEMENT ANNOUNCED on October 23, 1945, that I had been signed and would be sent to their Montreal farm club in the International League, it created a furor in the world of sports. Mr. Rickey, his subordinates, and I had all expected the lid to blow off and, believe me, it did.

Before the announcement was made, Mr. Rickey cautioned me: "Don't act excited," he said. "Just be yourself. Simply say that you are going to do the best you can to make good and let it go at that."

That crisp October day in the offices of the Montreal Royals, I was ready and waiting when the big group of newspapermen came stalking into the office of Mr. Hector Racine, President of the club. In the papers the next day, they reported that I had been cool and had handled myself well during the interview. I may have created that impression, but actually I was nervous as the devil. I had never faced such a huge battery of writers, and I knew that every word I said would be recorded and then interpreted. The stories would be printed in papers throughout Canada and the United States. If I said the wrong thing or created the wrong impression, I would have the sportswriters and fans down on me. And that would just about finish me before I ever started. So I felt mighty good the next day when I read the favorable notices in the Montreal papers. It awed me, however, to discover that I had been appraised in much the same way as a new Broadway production is reviewed by the drama critics.

One of the best write-ups I got was from Al Parsley of the *Montreal Herald*. I will always be especially grateful to him for that article, even though he wrote many a good one about me after that. He was, in fact, one of my greatest boosters while I was playing for the Royals. This is what Al wrote the following day:

"There were many things about Jack Robinson which impressed you. He talked with that easy fluency of an educated man; then you remembered that he was a senior at the University of California in Los Angeles before he enlisted.

"You felt that somehow Jack Robinson was most sincere in his views on a problem that baseball men, big and little, have found no way of solving over many years. He has a great realization of his responsibilities, and he said without bravado: 'Maybe I'm doing something for my race.' When he said that, it was felt by one or two of his auditors that it was a speech that maybe Joe Louis could have made. Some remembered that Louis has always been a fine example of his people.

"At that, though of darker hue, Robinson looks slightly like Louis in general appearance. He has the same serious, near-sombre mein and he is so forthright in his ideals.

"He answered a dozen questions fired at him by the group of newsmen and radiomen with easy confidence, but no cocksureness nor bragadoccio.

"His was no easy chore at that. There were easily twenty-five press and radiomen in the room when Hector H. Racine made the startling announcement that the Montreal Baseball Club was the first to tear down the barriers, those invisible, but up-to-now fearsome roadblocks which prohibited the admittance of colored players into the ranks of organized baseball.

"He was a lone black man entering a room where the gathering, if not frankly hostile, was at least belligerently indifferent. He came in shyly, walking with the firm springy step which betokens the athlete, well-trained."

Parsley's column that day was typical of the others in the city of Montreal. The gentlemen of the Canadian press were willing to accept me on the basis of my ability. They made it easy for me by taking my signing in stride, and I was indeed grateful to them.

But reception of the news was by no means all favorable. As soon as the story hit the wires, storm clouds appeared in the South. The first, and perhaps most ominous, was an interview with Minor League Baseball Commissioner W. G. Bramham. (He has died since then, but at that time Mr. Bramham was very much alive and very powerful in the baseball world.) Jack Horner, Sports Editor of the Durham, North Carolina, *Herald,* interviewed Mr. Bramham. Among other things, the Commissioner said the following:

"Whenever I hear a white man [Branch Rickey], whether he be from the North, South, East, or West, broadcasting what a Moses he is to the Negro race, right then I know the latter needs a body guard.

"It is my opinion that if the Negro is left alone and aided by his own unselfish friends of the white race, he will work out his own salvation.

"It is those of the carpetbagger stripe of the white race, who, under the guise of helping but in truth using the Negro for their own selfish interest, retard the race. The Negro is making rapid strides in baseball as well as other lines of endeavor.

"They have their own form of player contracts and, as I understand it, their organizations are well officered and are financially successful. Why should we raid their ranks, grab a player, and put him, his baseball associates, and his race in a position that will inevitably prove harmful?

"When the Negro needs counsel, guidance, or assistance, from his white friends, he will let it be known and will be found meeting with a heavy response, unaccompanied by ostentation or trumpeting. . . .

"Father Divine will have to look to his laurels, for we can expect Rickey Temple to be in the course of construction in Harlem soon."

But Mr. Bramham had to admit that there was nothing he could do about this unique situation. He had to admit there was no law in organized baseball prohibiting the employment of a Negro. "Nothing else appearing that I know of," he said, "Robinson's contract will be promulgated just as any other contract. This is a matter, insofar as our rules are concerned, which is left entirely with individual leagues and their clubs."

Although there was nothing he could do about it officially, Bramham had prepared the way for attack by those groups and individuals who were opposed to the move.

In all baseball history there had never been so much divided opinion on the signing of one lone ball player. Remember now, I was not signing to play in the Big Leagues — I was simply being given a trial in a Minor League club. And there was no certainty on anyone's part, including mine, that I would make the grade.

One man who did not seem to be upset about it was Mr. Frank Shaughnessy, president of the International League. He apparently took it in stride when he told the Associated Press:

"There's no rule in baseball that says a Negro can't play with a club in organized ball. As long as any fellow's the right type and can make good and can get along with other players, he can play ball. I don't think that much prejudice exists any longer. I believe such things are more political than social now."

That certainly was encouraging. I learned later, however, that Mr. Shaughnessy was apprehensive over what might happen when I played in Baltimore — a Southern city.

Horace Stoneham, President of the New York Giants, was also optimistic. "That's really a fine way to start the program," he said. "We will scout the Negro Leagues next year, looking for young prospects. However, the primary responsibility we have is to find a place for our returning servicemen, numbering into the hundreds, and only if they prove incapable will new players be placed on our clubs."

I was glad Mr. Stoneham approved, but I was puzzled by his reference to returning servicemen. Had he forgotten that there were Negro veterans? Maybe he didn't know it at the time, but I was a returning serviceman, too. I had been a lieutenant in the United States Army and had an honorable discharge. However, the important thing was that Mr. Stoneham would also consider Negro players.

William Benswanger, President of the Pittsburgh Pirates, was very brief and noncommittal. "It is an affair of the Brooklyn and Montreal Clubs," he said, "whom they may sign, whether white or colored."

Mr. Benswanger doubtless felt he had to speak cautiously. Several years previously he had promised Wendell Smith of the *Pittsburgh Courier* that he would give three Negro players tryouts. He had been, in fact, the first owner to announce publicly that he would consider Negro players. When Smith selected three players and took them to Benswanger, the Pirates' owner had backed down. He knew, I guess, that a lot of people would remember that he had changed his mind when the decision had actually been dropped in his lap.

Some baseball men were actually awe-stricken when they learned that Montreal had signed a Negro. Such was

st have been destined to play for Leo Durocher, because I immediately started
awking when I was born. By the time I was four, as pictured above, I had learned
rin, too.

My mother was the sole support of our family. When we were kids we had a constant struggle to make ends meet. On the left is my brother Mack, who later became a great athlete at the University of Oregon. He has his arm around me (age six). Next is Edgar, then Willa Mae and Frank.

Some of the fellows asked me to give them a few hints on how I hold a bat and swing it. When I was a kid I wanted to be a coach, and later on I did coach a team at a small Negro college in Texas.

Since I could fake pretty well, I was used as the man-in-motion on offense at UCLA. As half-back, I had a ball-carrying average of about 12 yards per try.

Basketball was also one of my favorite sports. In the seasons of 1940 and 1941 I played forward for UCLA and led the Southern Division of the Pacific Coast Conference in scoring with 281 points for the two years, an average of 12 points per game.

At UCLA, I was more interested in football than any other sport. Here I am circling right end against the Huskies of the University of Washington on November 23, 1940. Don Means (32) and Ray Frankowski (34) of Washington are converging on me.

Kenny Washington (8) was my team-mate in both basketball and football at UCLA. Kenny was almost unanimous choice for All-American on the gridiron and I was named on a number of All-American teams. Our basketball coach was Wilbur Johns.

Track events held more interest for me in college than did baseball. I broke the junior college broad-jump record held by my brother Mack, by leaping 25 feet, 6⅓ inches, as against his 25 feet.

I met Rachel Isum when we were both studying at UCLA. Without her help and encouragement I would never have reached the Major Leagues. We were married in 1946. This was one of the few occasions when I consented to get dressed in formal clothes.

41

I went into the Army in 1942 and was commissioned a second lieutenant a year later. In November 1944, I received my Army discharge and the following spring joined the Kansas City Monarchs as a shortstop.

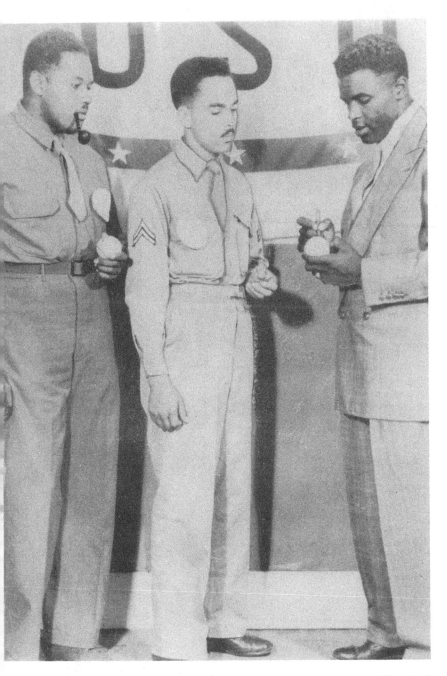

When I got out of the Service the fellows wanted me to autograph baseballs wherever I went.

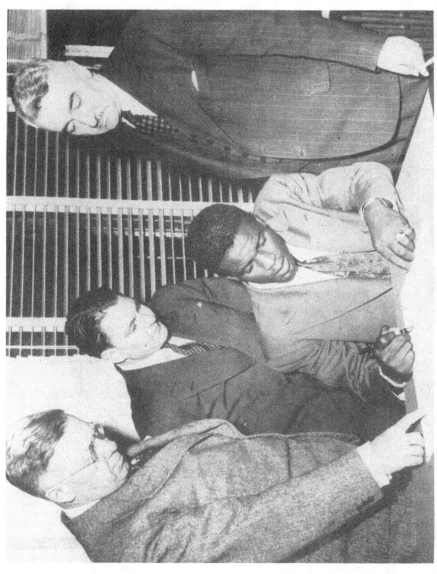

This was one of the proudest moments of my life, signing a contract with the Montreal Royals of the International League, farm club of the Dodgers. Looking on (left to right) Mr. Hector Racine, President of the Royals, Mr. Branch Rickey, Jr., and Mr. J. Romeo Gauvreau.

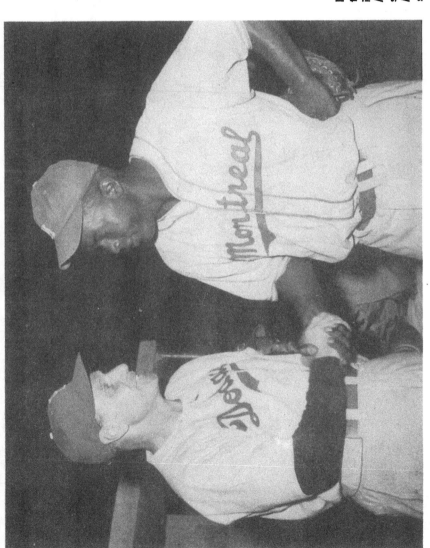

I met Leo Durocher for the first time when I was in spring training with Montreal. When I first signed with the Dodgers, Mr. Durocher had been suspended for a year.

45

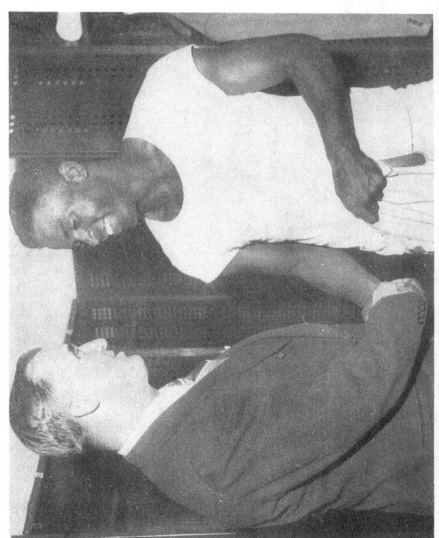

Happy Chandler, Commissioner of Baseball, never had to make a decision on my contract dispute between the Dodgers and the Kansas City Monarchs. The owner of the Monarchs dropped his demands. I never had signed a contract, anyway.

Here are some of my closest pals in the Negro sports world. On my left are Wendell Smith, sportswriter for the Chicago Herald-American and the *Pittsburgh Courier*; Duke Slater, Iowa's All-American tackle; Ralph Metcalfe, famous Marquette sprinter.

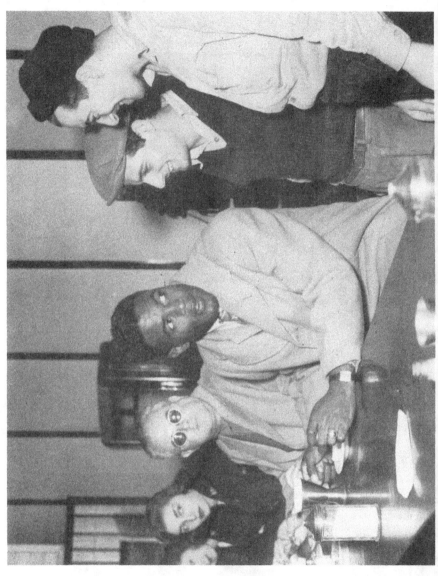

Wherever I go people are friendly. Here a couple of truck drivers have stopped to talk over the baseball situation while I grab a bite to eat.

Joseph Brown, Secretary of the Buffalo Bisons. "Very surprising," he said. "It's hard to believe — I can't understand it."

The issue was so full of dynamite that a number of prominent people refused to comment on it. Among them was Baseball's Commissioner, Happy Chandler.

When the story broke, Mr. Chandler was in New York to speak at a luncheon of The Saints and Sinners in honor of Hank Greenberg. Baseball writers, of course, immediately asked his opinion of the step. "I have nothing to say either way," he said.

Meanwhile, down in Dallas, Texas, another executive, President Alvin Gardner of the Texas League, issued the following statement: "I'm positive you'll never see any Negro players on any of the teams in organized baseball in the South as long as the Jim Crow laws are in force."

The comment of Eddie Collins, General Manager of the Boston Red Sox, was particularly interesting to me. "Robinson worked out for us last spring. Very few players can step into the Majors from college or sandlot baseball. Of course, they always have a chance to prove themselves in the Minors. More power to Robinson if he can make the grade."

Mr. Alva Bradley, then President of the Cleveland Indians, made a pointed observation that was absolutely true. He said: "That's the only way colored boys will ever get into the Major Leagues — by breaking in with Minor League teams and proving they have the ability to play Major League ball. Colored boys have never been discriminated against in the Major Leagues. They have simply never been able to get into Minor Leagues to get the proper training for Major League competition."

From all this, I concluded there would be no concerted effort to keep me out. Some men didn't object to my being signed with Montreal; others, though they disapproved, admitted they couldn't do anything about it.

49

*W**hose Property?*

THERE WAS, HOWEVER, ANOTHER STUMBLING BLOCK THAT was causing concern: what — if any — legal claims did the Kansas City Monarchs of the Negro American League have on me?

No sooner had I signed the contract with Montreal when charges that Branch Rickey was a "Thief, Robber, and Burglar!" came pouring out of Kansas City.

When I had played shortstop for the Kansas City Monarchs in 1945, I had hit in the neighborhood of .350 and had been selected to play in the celebrated East-West Game. (Patterned after the Major League All-Star Game, it is a contest between the best players in the two Negro baseball leagues.) It was my first year in professional baseball and I guess the owners of the Monarchs considered me a valuable asset. In any event, when they discovered that I had been whisked away by Brooklyn and was about to enter organized baseball, they hit the ceiling.

The owners of the team, J. L. Wilkinson and Tom Baird — both of whom, incidentally, are fine men — immediately claimed me as their property and put a price on my whirling head. Just two days after the news broke, Baird declared: "We won't take it lying down. Robinson signed a contract with us last year and I feel that he is our property. If Chandler lets Montreal and Brooklyn get by with this, he's really starting a mess."

Happy Chandler had been Commissioner of Baseball

50

but a short time when this happened. He was already engaged in a number of disputes with various people in baseball, and a number of sportswriters were howling for his scalp. It was apparent that he was not going to welcome this new altercation. A lot of people were ready to criticize any decisions he might make.

I don't imagine Chandler ever dreamed that he would be called on to adjudicate between the Negro Leagues, now threatened with what they considered wholesale raiding, and the teams of organized (white) baseball, which hired him. In fact, I think Wilkinson's and Baird's reaction was a big surprise to almost everybody. I know that I had taken it for granted that Negro Baseball would universally hail the event as the long-sought opening wedge into the Big Leagues. But Wilkinson and Baird — who, by the way, are white men — were anything but pleased by the news. And their cries of protest penetrated to the usually tranquil shores of the historic Potomac in Washington, D. C.

Not only has Clark Griffith successfully operated the Washington Senators for years, but he has also made a respectable sum by renting his ball park to such Negro teams as the Homestead Grays. From 1940 to 1945, the Grays, with their famous home-run-hitting catcher, the late Josh Gibson, drew fine crowds to Griffith Stadium. It is not farfetched to suppose that the rent Griffith received from the Grays in one season paid the salaries of almost half his ball club. Presumably, he had no desire to further any move that might threaten the existence of so lucrative an institution as Negro Baseball.

When he signed me, Mr. Rickey had the following to say about Negro baseball contracts: "There are a number of colored teams, with more or less fixed identities, throughout the country and none of these is a member of any league whatsoever — in the sense of a 'league' in organized baseball. There is at the present time, so far as

51

I know, no league or association of clubs that has a constitution or rules and regulations. There has been no uniform contract for players; every player is a free agent at the end of the current season. No club or league anywhere is incorporated."

He went on to say that he had investigated the operations of the Negro Leagues and they were in the nature of a racket. Anyone familiar with the operations of the Negro Leagues had to agree with him—all but the owners of teams in these Leagues, who, naturally, considered it an unfair charge. Space will not permit me to go into detail in this particular phase of baseball, but everything Mr. Rickey said in that statement was true.

When Branch Rickey issued his observation on Negro Leagues, Clark Griffith put on his hip boots and waded into the controversy. He challenged Rickey's right to set himself up as "dictator" of Negroes in baseball. "Mr. Rickey is attempting to destroy two well-organized Leagues," he told the Associated Press. "These Leagues have been in existence for some time, and the Negro people of this country have faith and confidence in them. This is not the age of dictators, and when one man sets himself up to foster the new organization [at that time Rickey was planning to organize what he hoped would be a real Negro league], which only has in mind the thought of destroying the existing two Negro Leagues, then I think the time has arrived when a halt should be called.

"If the Brooklyn Dodgers want Robinson, they should pay for him. . . . While it is true that we have no agreement with the Negro Leagues — National and American — we still can't act like outlaws in taking their stars. We have no right to destroy them. If Brooklyn wants to buy Robinson from Kansas City, that is all right, but contracts of Negro teams should be recognized by organized baseball.

"In the eyes of organized baseball, the Negro teams today should have the same status as Minor Leagues before the draft went into effect. We bought their players in those days on the basis of the highest bid."

Griffith concluded by saying that Commisioner Chandler should do something about my case if the presidents of the Negro Leagues asked him to rule on it.

Now Mr. Griffith's sudden and intense interest in my particular case was somewhat surprising in the light of his past attitude toward Negro ball players. His ball park is situated in the heart of Washington's Negro district, and thousands of Negroes are faithful Washington fans. They had repeatedly urged him to hire Negro players, but he had never done so. He had dispatched his scouts to neighboring countries such as Mexico and Cuba to find ball players to improve his club, but he wouldn't sign a Negro.

His Negro tenants, the Homestead Grays, were the Negro champions of baseball, and he saw them play many a week end; yet not even the prodigious clouts of Josh Gibson were enough to make him forget the color line. (After seeing Gibson play one time, no less an authority than Walter Johnson estimated that Gibson would be worth 200,000 dollars to any Big League Club.) Griffith would hire dark-complexioned Cubans, Mexicans, and players from other Latin countries. Few of them could speak English and none of them had been American citizens for any length of time, but Clark Griffith for some reason considered them more acceptable than Negro Americans.

Consequently, the Negro public was not unduly moved by Mr. Griffith's professed concern over Negro baseball. He was most assuredly not their chosen mouthpiece.

Branch Rickey was quick in replying to Griffith's attack, and the verbal battle was growing hot when suddenly the Kansas City owners, Baird and Wilkinson, did

53

an about-face. They must have realized that, as owners of a Negro ball club, they were making a serious mistake in protesting the advancement of a Negro player to organized baseball, no matter what technicalities they might have in their favor. Their protest had certainly not been applauded by Negro fans across the country. The average Negro, I think, reasoned thus: "Why all the fuss about Robinson? Kansas City can get another shortstop, but this may be the only chance for Negroes to break into organized baseball. If they block this move of Rickey's, it may never happen again. If the Monarchs stop Rickey from getting Robinson, then I'll stop going to see their team play."

They also reasoned that two white men had no right, in the name of defending Negro baseball, to block a move so full of promise for Negro athletes.

In any event, Mr. Baird told the *Kansas City Star* that the Monarchs would in no way attempt to prevent me from playing with Montreal. He said all plans to appeal to Commissioner Chandler had been dismissed. And Mr. Wilkinson announced that he was positive that I could not only make the grade in the International League, but that I would burn it up. "We want him to go into organized baseball and make good," Wilkinson said. "He is a fine ball player and a real gentleman. He's a sure bet to make the Majors."

That ended it all right there. I must say, however, that if the Monarchs had called upon Commissioner Chandler, they could not have presented much of an argument. They could not have shown him a bonafide contract since I never signed one. The secretary of the club wrote me before the season started and invited me to join the team. I accepted, informing him that I would report within the next few days. When I joined the team in Texas that spring, I just started playing. I was never offered a contract. I simply agreed to play for a stipulated amount and that was all there was to it.

Yet even though a formal protest and hearing would most certainly have been a dud, I was relieved when the sound and fury subsided. It made it a lot easier for me to concentrate on winning a regular berth on the Montreal team.

*T*he Press Goes to Bat

THE SPORTSWRITERS, MORE THAN ANY OTHER GROUP OR individual, are responsible for the entry of Negro players into organized baseball. For years and years they have fought for the abolishment of the color line. Never have they let baseball's officialdom forget that as long as they barred any race, creed, or color from the diamond, baseball could not be called the American sport.

It is no secret that for years there was a tacit understanding among owners in organized baseball that the Negro player was taboo. He was not barred constitutionally, but it was definitely understood that he was not to be signed.

The owners assumed that if they said nothing about accepting Negro players, the issue would die a natural death.

The technique was successful for many, many years, but the agitation to hire Negro players never died out. In fact, it mounted steadily. Sportswriters from coast to coast kept hammering away at the seemingly impregnable wall. Public support grew stronger and stronger. At last cracks began to appear, and then the barrier was smashed. I happened to be the first player to benefit.

As far back as 1888, twelve years after the National League was organized, the fight to admit Negro players to the Major Leagues was already under way. Leading the campaign was the now defunct Detroit *Plaindealer*. The following is typical of the paper's attitude:

"The *Plaindealer* desires to see the League members give such star players as 'Fleet' Walker, Higgins, Grant ('The Black Dunlap'), Stovey, Fowler, and other Afro-Americans a chance to fill the weak places in the League teams. Since Afro-Americans can and do play a stiff game, and hundreds of their race give substantial support to the National League, this, it seems to us, would be but fair and right."

The players referred to were all starring with small clubs outside the National League. Three of them — Stovey, Higgins, and Walker — became principals in what was probably the first racial flare-up on record in professional baseball. The episode set the precedent for the long-continued ban against Negro players. It occurred around the turn of the century. At that time the three Negro stars were playing with Newark of the International League. Manager Eason of Chicago, a National League club, refused to play a scheduled game with Newark if the latter used its Negro players. The Newark manager refused to bench Stovey, Higgins, and Walker; and Chicago walked off the field. Later on, some of the Southern players on the Newark team refused to have pictures taken with their Negro teammates, and shortly afterward the Negro players were traded to Syracuse.

These events inspired a number of other papers across the country to join the Detroit *Plaindealer* in objecting to the exclusion of Negroes from professional baseball. Over the years a growing proportion of the press took up the crusade of molding public opinion. And without the pressure and support of the fans and public, no owner could or would have been able to take the initial step.

One of the men who fought doggedly for the entry of Negroes into the ranks of organized baseball was the late and beloved Damon Runyon. Probably the most

gifted sportswriter of our time, Runyon abhorred the
ban against Negro players. For instance, in May of 1945,
before I was signed by Montreal, he wrote:

"I read a statement in a newspaper the other day that
baseball belongs to all the people. This may be true of
baseball as a vacant-lot pastime, but it is definitely not
true of organized or professional baseball, and it is sheer
hypocrisy to say that it does.

"If baseball belonged to all the people and the people
had a vote in its conduct, Negroes would be permitted to
play in organized baseball if they could make good by the
same standards set for the whites.

"Track and field sports and professional and amateur
boxing are pretty much dominated by Americans of Negro
ancestry. In international competition such as the Olympic Games our nation eagerly proclaims the exploits of
these Americans as national triumphs, and in boxing the
presence of Negro participants does not keep the attend-
ance from being larger than ever before in history or
reduce the number of whites willing to compete against
the Negroes.

"I do not see why baseball should be more exclusive
than track and field and boxing and college football
when it comes to the participation of Negroes."

Another top-flight sportswriter who was in the thick of
the fight along with Runyon and the others was Dan
Parker of the New York *Daily Mirror*. In one of his many
columns on the subject he wrote: "There is no good
reason why, in a country that calls itself a democracy,
intolerance should exist on the sports field, most democratic of all meeting places. Nor does it exist in many
branches of sport besides baseball. The Negro is welcomed in college football except in the South. No one
will claim that the game has ever suffered through having
welcomed players like Paul Robeson, the Rutgers All-
American star. Boxing has never been more respectable

than it has been during the reign of Joe Louis. Some of our greatest college players have been Negro boys. Track and field records scintillate with the performances of dark-skinned athletes; but the Satchel Paiges and Josh Gibsons must stick to their own leagues — except when they want to pay to see how the white boys do it.

"Baseball is hypocritical in the extreme on the Negro question. The club owners have always welcomed Negroes — at the box office. Some have given out statements (when requested) fairly vibrating with inter-racial goodwill, but to get the game's real attitude toward the color line, you must put a baseball man on the spot. Then the truth comes out."

It was such outright punches, thrown by influential writers, that finally made it possible for me to get into organized baseball. He was not pleading for me personally, of course; it just so happened that I turned out to be the guinea pig.

Warren Brown, dean of Chicago's baseball writers and a member of the sports staff of the Chicago *Herald American*, was also outspoken on the subject. In December of 1943 he wrote:

"It seems to me that the tears of some of the organized baseball operators over the dearth of playing material might be wiped away were this obvious [Negro Leagues] and always apparent source of supply tapped.

"In these times, more than ever before, the employment of a Negro player by an organized baseball club is not something to be regarded as a radical move, but rather one actuated by common sense."

Two days after I had signed to play with Montreal, Red Smith, now with the New York *Herald Tribune*, wrote in the Philadelphia *Record*: "In the words of the old spiritual, 'everybody talk about Heaven ain't goin' there,' and it has become unbeautifully apparent these last few days that not everybody who prattles of toler

59

ance and racial equality has precisely the same understanding of the terms.

"Since the Montreal club, a Brooklyn farm, overstepped baseball's unwritten Jim Crow policy by signing Jackie Robinson, a Negro infielder, there has been a fancy assortment of public statements of baseball men.

"Consider the views expressed, starting with that of Washington's Clark Griffith. Now that positive action has been taken, Griff suddenly emerges as the defender of the American Negro League's property rights. It is not on record that Griff ever concerned himself with the property rights of the Cuban and South American teams whence he drew material.

"If he [Robinson] has the guts and ability to stick it out until he can win acceptance in all quarters outside of baseball, he'll have no difficulties in the clubhouse. There is more democracy in the locker room than on the street.

"And that's the truth."

Another famous sportswriter who was in my corner — and the corner of all Negro players — was Bill Corum of the New York *Journal American*. In his column of October 26, 1945, Mr. Corum wrote:

"To make a *cause célèbre* of the matter, to stir a tempest in a teapot; can do nothing or nobody, including the Negro race, baseball, Chandler, the Rickeys, and in the end, most important of all, our country, anything save harm.

"Professional boxing hasn't too many stars in its crown. But in this matter it has been so far ahead of baseball as to be almost in another world.

"Members of all races and from all sorts of places have been meeting together in the ring on a may-the-best-man-win basis for so long that people with any sense at all have ceased to give it a second thought.

"It won't be many years until the same will be true of Negroes playing in organized baseball. Some day the big leagues (though it is doubtful if Robinson at twenty-six can climb the hill) must be that way if the National Pastime is to continue to be a sport in sports-loving America."

One of the best pieces was written by Dave Egan of the Boston *Record* in 1943. I was in the Service then, but I later came to know him and regard him as one of my closest friends.

"We are fighting, as I understand it," Dave wrote, "for the rights of underprivileged peoples everywhere. We weep for the teeming masses of India. Down the years, we must have contributed millions to the suffering Armenians. We have room in our souls to pity the Chinese, and the Arabs, and the brave Greeks. Could we, by any chance, spare a thought for the Negro in the United States? Do we, by any chance, feel disgust at the thought that Negro athletes, solely because of their color, are barred from playing baseball?"

Another influential writer who kept hammering at the Major League doors was Gordon Macker of the Los Angeles *Daily News*. "With some of the pitiful baseball exhibitions that are being staged in ball parks all over the country because of the talent shortage, it doesn't make sense why Negro players aren't given a break. . . .

"If a boy from 43rd and Central is good enough to stop a bullet in France, he's good enough to stop a line drive at 42nd and Avalon."

While most sportswriters strongly agitated for the admission of Negro players to the Majors, there were some who were opposed — not for any bigoted reasons, but because the prospect seemed so hopeless or so charged with dynamite.

Jimmy Powers of the New York *Daily News* predicted that I would fail to make the grade. He might well have been right, but the way he arrived at his prediction revealed a rather large blind spot. Here is what Mr. Powers wrote: "Jackie Robinson, the Negro signed by Brooklyn, will not make the grade in the Big Leagues next year or the next, if percentages mean anything. Every Major League ball club has a backlog of young talent, proven stars, returning from the war. Some Big League clubs, like the Cards and Brooklyns, really have material for two teams. All clubs under the GI Bill of Rights must pay their returning Big Leaguers one year's salary at the same scale they received before they went to war.

"Robinson would have to be a super player to 'bump' a returning veteran. We would like to see him make good, but it is unfair to build high hopes and then dash them down. . . . Robinson is a 1000-1 shot to make the grade.

"If the Negro player couldn't muscle into the Major League line-ups when forty-three-year-old outfielders patrolled the grass for pennant winners and one-armed men and callow 4F's were stumbling around, he won't make it in 1946 when the rosters will be bursting with returned headliners, all competent Big Leaguers of proven ability."

In other words, Mr. Powers implied that Negroes were simply not good enough to make a Major League club even in wartime. The truth of the matter was that the Major Leagues did not relax their barriers and give Negro players a chance even when "forty-three-year-old outfielders patrolled the grass. . . ."

The fact that Powers' prediction that I would not make the grade proved to be wrong was significant only because it demonstrated that, given the opportunity, Negroes could play Major League ball.

Stanley Frank, formerly of the New York *Post*, professed great concern for the welfare of any Negro player who might manage to climb to the Majors. In July of 1942 he wrote: "I tell you I want to see Negroes in the Big Leagues, . . . but not under present conditions. . . . I tell you this because I know Southern ball players will brandish sharp spikes with intent to cut and maim Negro infielders; that there will be an unprecedented wave of murderous bean-balls thrown at Negro batters; that jockeying from the benches will descend to subhuman levels of viciousness."

I suppose Mr. Frank's strong premonitions were all possibilities. Yet I've been in organized baseball two years now, and I've played with and against lots of Southerners. I haven't been beaned; I haven't been intentionally maimed; and, in my opinion, the jockeying from the benches has not descended to "subhuman levels of viciousness."

The demand for entry of Negro players into organized baseball had been the subject of innumerable articles by Negro sportswriters for many years. All agreed that something should be done but no method for breaking the race barriers was evolved until 1945 when the Fair Employment Practices Commission came into being in New York State.

In February 1945, Chick Solomon, former ball player and well-known sports photographer, walked into the Hotel Theresa in New York City while the National Negro League club owners were in session. He had just returned from Albany where he had photographed the signing of the FEPC bill by Governor Thomas E. Dewey.

"Now that we have a legal document to back us up," Solomon said, "what is there to keep any qualified Negro from walking in with spikes and gloves to a Major League training camp and demanding a tryout?" It happened that, due to travel restrictions, the Dodgers were then in spring training up north at Bear Mountain, fifty miles from New York City. "We need a good man to make the test," Solomon suggested, "and Ray Campanella is the man." However, my friend Ray was in Baltimore and could not make the trip.

Joe Bostic, then sports editor of the *People's Voice,*

63

Negro weekly, caught on to the idea and shortly afterwards corralled Terris McDuffie, a pitcher, and Showboat Thomas, captain and fancy-dan first baseman of the New York Cubans, for a trip to Bear Mountain. Without previous notice, Bostic and the two players barged in and demanded a tryout from Branch Rickey. Mr. Rickey graciously consented to a tryout on the following day. The two players were permitted to don their uniforms next day and they worked out under Mr. Rickey's eyes. After the trial, Mr. Rickey said he would have to hold his decision in abeyance until he had time to set the machinery in motion that would make it possible for a qualified Negro to be offered a contract by the Dodgers.

Mr. Rickey decided then that the Negro leagues were worth watching and he sent qualified scouts out to round up Negro players. It was later that season that Clyde Sukeforth contacted me in Chicago; so I was the lucky guy who benefited by all this ground work.

True, there is still discrimination in America, and indignities are by no means limited to the world of baseball — as any Negro can testify. Some of us have to break the ice. And I have found that most players and fans are, if not actually pulling for me, at least neither hostile nor vicious. That fact I attribute largely to the ceaseless efforts of a whole army of outspoken sportswriters who have preached fair play and democracy.

Florida Welcome

MY FIRST YEAR IN ORGANIZED BASEBALL WAS PROBABLY the most crucial one in my life. It was the year I was sent to Montreal, and when it was over I was sure that I could make the grade in the Majors. I wasn't cocky, mind you, just confident; for in that year I learned a lot of things, the most important of which was that ball players — whether they came from the South or North — would accept me and play with me.

That was in 1946 and we were to train at Daytona Beach, Florida. With my wife I left Los Angeles late in February by plane. As we flew over the Western deserts, I wondered just how I would get along down in the deep South. Everyone knows that the Southern states have placed numerous restrictions upon the liberties of Negroes. It was going to be a comparatively new experience for me, and I wasn't sure what to expect.

We had a tough time getting to Daytona Beach. At one point we had to give up our seats because the Army still had priority on planes. So we took a train to Jacksonville, and when we got there we found we'd have to go the rest of the way by bus. We didn't like the bus, and we particularly didn't like the back seat when there were empty seats near the center. Florida law designates where Negroes are to ride in public conveyances. The law says: "Back seat." We rode there.

When we arrived in Daytona Beach we were met at

the bus station by Wendell Smith, sports editor of *The Pittsburgh Courier,* and Billy Rowe, a photographer for the same paper. They had been there about four days and had arranged housing accommodations and other necessities. With them was Johnny Wright, a good friend of mine and a pitcher for the Homestead Grays of the Negro National League. Mr. Rickey had signed Johnny to a Montreal contract not long after he had signed me. Johnny had come up with a good record in the Negro National League and had been a star pitcher for a Navy team in 1945.

They took us to the home of a prominent Negro family. The rest of the team usually stayed at a big hotel on the ocean front, but this particular time they were quartered at Sanford, Florida, where the Dodger organization was looking over at least two hundred players.

As a result of our transportation difficulties, I was two days late. I learned from Smith and Rowe that Mr. Rickey was a bit upset about my late arrival; so we decided to get up early next morning and drive to Sanford, which is some twenty miles south of Daytona Beach.

We arrived in Sanford the next morning about ten o'clock, but instead of going to the ball park, we decided to go to the home of Mr. Brock, a well-to-do Negro citizen of the town, and call Mr. Rickey. We had to feel our way in this entire matter. We didn't want to cause a commotion or upset anything by walking into the park and surprising everyone. It was no secret that Johnny and I were going to be there, but we felt it best to remain as inconspicuous as possible.

Smith called Mr. Rickey at his hotel and he told us we should get over to the park as soon as possible. We took our shoes and gloves and hurried over. Clyde Suke-forth met us. We shook hands. "Go right into the dressing room and get your uniforms," he said. "Babe Hamburger, our clubhouse man, is in there. He'll see that you get fixed up."

I glanced at the players on the field. They had come from every section of the country — two hundred men out there, all hoping some day to become members of the Brooklyn Dodgers. Some were tossing balls to each other; others were hitting fungoes to the outfielders; still others were running around the field conditioning their legs. Suddenly I felt uncomfortably conspicuous standing there. Every single man on the field seemed to be staring at Johnny Wright and me. . . .

We ducked into the clubhouse. It was empty save for one man, a big, fat fellow. I felt a bit tense and I'm sure Johnny did, too. We were ill at ease and didn't know exactly what to do next. The man saw us then and came right over and introduced himself. "Hiya, fellows," he said with a big, broad smile on his face. "I'm Babe Hamburger. . . . Robinson and Wright, eh? Well, that's swell. Which one is Robinson?"

I put out my hand and he gave it a hearty shake. "This is Johnny Wright," I said. Johnny shook Babe's big, soft mitt.

"Well, fellows," he said, "I'm not exactly what you'd call a part of this great experiment, but I'm gonna give you some advice anyway. Just go out there and do your best. Don't get tense. Just be yourselves."

Be ourselves? Here in the heart of the race-conscious South? . . . Johnny and I both realized that this was hostile territory — that anything could happen any time to a Negro who thought he could play ball with white men on an equal basis. It was going to be difficult to relax and behave naturally. But we assured Babe we'd try. . . . He was grand to us. I'll never forget that jolly disposition and winning smile.

We finally got dressed and headed for the field. Waiting for us was a group of reporters from New York, Pittsburgh, Baltimore, Montreal, and Brooklyn. They surrounded us and started firing questions:

"What are you going to do if the pitchers start throwing at you?" one of them asked.

"The same thing everyone else does," I answered, smiling. "Duck!"

Someone asked me if I'd like to play with the Dodgers.

"I certainly hope to someday," I said.

"What about Pee Wee Reese?" another asked.

"I'm not worried about Reese," I said with a firm note in my voice. "I haven't even made the Montreal team yet."

"Do you think you're good enough to play with Brooklyn now?" the Brooklyn writer asked.

"I don't know if I'm good enough to play with Montreal," I said. "So I'm not even thinking about Brooklyn."

After they had asked us questions about everything under the sun, we were rescued by Sukeforth. "Come on," he said, "I want you to meet Clay Hopper, the manager of the club."

Clay Hopper is from Mississippi. We had often wondered before the training camp drills got under way if Hopper would be willing to accept us. Would he actually help us, or would he bench us? A number of newspapers had asked the same questions.

Hopper was standing near the dugout when we walked up. "Clay," said Sukeforth, "this is Robinson and Wright."

"Hello, Jackie," Hopper said. We shook hands.

"Hello, Johnny," he said to Wright. "Have a nice winter rest?" he asked us.

We both said we had.

Speaking with a typical, soft Southern drawl, Hopper

said, "Well, we aren't going to do much today. Just throw the ball around and hit a few. . . . You're a shortstop, aren't you, Jackie?"

"Well, that's what I played at Kansas City," I answered, smiling. "I hope I'm good enough to be one at Montreal."

"What's your best pitch?" he asked Johnny.

"Well," Wright answered, speaking deliberately, "I'd say my fast ball."

"He's got a dandy curve, too," I said quickly.

"Got a change-up?" asked Hopper.

A "change-up" in baseball terminology is a change-of-pace ball. Pitchers use the pitch to get batters off balance. It is one pitch that all pitchers in the Brooklyn organization must develop.

"I can throw a change-up," Johnny said, "but I didn't have to use it much in the league I played in last season."

"You'll need it in this league," Hopper advised him. "So when you start throwing today, practice it."

It was hard to determine whether or not Hopper resented our being assigned to his club. He was certainly giving Johnny some good advice and he talked pleasantly to both of us, but he could simply be acting the role of a good officer following orders. The tone of his voice revealed nothing one way or the other. The only thing I noticed was that his comments and instructions were given quickly and sharply.

The players were on both sides of the diamond tossing the ball back and forth. Sukeforth walked over along the third base side and picked out two of them. He introduced us. I can't recall their names now, but they seemed to be nice guys.

"You toss with these fellows," Sukey said.

He took Johnny farther down where the pitchers were working.

I was constantly interrupted by photographers. They took pictures of me throwing, catching, running, and sliding. I didn't mind, however, because it broke the monotony of just throwing the ball back and forth.

After an hour of that, we all were sent across the street from the park for batting practice. There was a big field there and a batting cage. There was also a pitching machine — a contraption that shoots a ball at the plate like a bullet. We all later agreed that it was of little value in improving our hitting. It did, however, save the pitchers.

When my turn to swing came, I hit a couple of long ones. I remember noticing one of the players standing around the cage roll his eyes and give a nod of approval. I felt as happy as a youngster showing off in front of some other boys.

Finally Hopper called a halt to proceedings. "That's enough for today," he said. "All of you be here at the same time in the morning."

That night we sat on the big porch of Mr. Brock's home and decided that it had been a good day. "Everyone was swell to us," I said, "and we were expecting a rather cool reception."

"Yeah," said Johnny, "it wasn't bad at all."

"You'll find good people every place you go," Mr. Brock said, stirring the ice in his glass of rum and cola. "Yes, sir, even here in Florida."

The next morning we were up bright and early. We went out to the park in a taxi and this time dressed with the rest of the players. Practice that day was a bit long, but not at all strenuous.

When we got back to Brock's, Johnny and I found Wendell Smith and Billy Rowe, our newspaper friends from Pittsburgh, waiting for us. Usually, they joked and kidded with us a lot; but that night they were both exceptionally quiet and sober. We all ate together. The conversation dragged until I began to feel uncomfortable. One or twice it seemed to me Smith and Rowe were exchanging significant glances, as though they had bad news they didn't want to announce in front of Johnny and me. I decided that maybe we had put our foot in it somehow or other and that they were angry at us. Why don't they say so, I thought. We're all friends, aren't we?

Rowe got up from the table suddenly and said to Smith, "I'm going to fill up with gas." He had a red Pontiac that he used to cover his assignments.

"We should be able to get out of here in fifteen or twenty minutes," Smith said. "Daytona isn't far, either."

"You guys leaving us?" I asked curiously.

"No," Smith said. "We're all going to Daytona."

Johnny and I looked at them in amazement. Were they losing their minds?

"Well," Smith said quickly, "don't just sit there. Pack your duds, fellows. We're blowin'."

"What about practice in the morning?" I asked. "After all, we came here to make the Montreal Club."

I was angry. What was this all about, anyway? No one had told us to move on to Daytona. Smith and Rowe didn't run the Brooklyn organization — nor did they run us, either. After all, things had been going beautifully. The first two days of practice had passed without a single incident. Surely we weren't being rejected after only a two-day trial! We were just beginning to loosen up a bit. The tenseness was going away. I was beginning to feel free and good inside.

As I sat there getting sorer by the minute, I heard Smith talking on the telephone: "Yes, Mr. Rickey," he said, "I'm with them now. We're pulling out for Daytona in about twenty minutes. Just as soon as they get their bags packed." I heard Rowe's car pull up in the driveway. Smith continued talking on the phone. "No," he said, "everything is okay now. It's just one of those things."

Just one of those things? What in the world was he talking about? Maybe Rickey had decided he wasn't going to keep us. Maybe this was the end and we were being sent home. I was boiling over now. I went upstairs and packed my bag. Suddenly I hated everything and everybody. I didn't care about the team or baseball or making good. All I wanted to do was get back home. I decided I would get my wife and head straight back to California. Rickey and Sukeforth had made a fool of me. "Damn 'em," I said under my breath.

We piled into the car and started for Daytona. Rowe was driving and Smith was sitting beside him. Johnny was in the back with me. None of us said a word. We stopped at the main intersection of the town for a traffic light. A group of men were standing on the street corner in their shirt sleeves. It looked like a typical small-town bull session.

I suddenly decided that Sanford wasn't a bad town at all. The people had been friendly to us. Apparently they liked ball players. The men on the corner turned to look at us. Easy-going guys, curious over where we were going — certainly not hostile, I thought. I smiled at them. I actually felt like waving.

Rowe broke the silence for the first time as the light changed and we picked up speed. "How can people like that call themselves Americans!" he said bitterly.

"They're as rotten as they come," Smith sneered.

"Now just a minute," I said. "They haven't done anything to us. They're nice people as far as I'm concerned."

"They sure are," Johnny agreed. "As far as I can tell, they liked us."

"Yeah," Smith said, swinging around and looking us in the face. His eyes were blazing with anger. "Sure, they liked you. They were in love with you. . . . That's why we're leaving."

"What do you mean?" I asked.

"I don't get it," chimed in Johnny.

"You will," Rowe said. "You will."

"Look," Smith said, "we didn't want to tell you guys because we didn't want to upset you. We want you to make this ball club. But . . . we're leaving this town because we've been told to get out. They won't stand for Negro ball players on the same field with whites!"

"Tell Him Ah Said to Git!"

THE EXPULSION FROM SANFORD WAS A HUMILIATING EXPERI-
ence. I found myself wishing I had never gotten mixed
up in the whole business. When the club moved into
Daytona, our permanent training base, what hope was
there that I would not be kicked out of town just as I had
been in Sanford? I was sure that as soon as I walked out
on the field, an objection would be raised. I didn't want
to go through that all over again. What could I do? Quit?
. . . I wanted to; but I just didn't have the nerve to walk
out on all the people who were counting on me — my
family and close friends, Mr. Rickey, the fourteen million
Negroes from coast to coast, the legion of understanding
white people. Dejected as I was, I just had to stick it out.

The rest of the team was quartered in a big hotel over-
looking the Atlantic Ocean. I stayed in the home of a
private family in the Negro section of the town. When we
finished practice, I'd go home and play cards with Smith,
Rowe, and my wife. Once in a while we'd go to a movie.
There was only one Negro movie in town and the picture
ran for three days. Consequently we'd see two pictures a
week. Often there was absolutely nothing to do. Our life
was so restricted and monotonous that sometimes we
would go to see the same movie twice.

Now and then some of the local Negroes would invite
us to dinner or for a game of cards. There was also a USO
Club near-by and some evenings I'd go there to play table

74

tennis or pinochle. But no matter how I tried I couldn't find a sufficient diversion to preoccupy me. I found myself stewing over the problems which I knew were bound to confront me sooner or later.

I had had no chance to know Clay Hopper, the manager of the Montreal team during my two-day stay in Sanford. When the club moved into Daytona Beach, I was anxious to find out just what kind of a guy he was. . . . Actually, I didn't want to know what kind of a guy *he* was — I wanted him to know what kind of a guy *I* was.

There were about twenty-five or thirty fellows on the Montreal squad. Many of them had played on the championship team the previous year, and I knew I was going to have a difficult time breaking into the line-up. I was listed as a shortstop and had to beat out at least three other men, including a wonderful little fellow by the name of Stanley Breard.

Breard had been the first-string shortstop in 1945 and had done a fine job. Not only that, Stan was a French-Canadian, born and reared in Montreal and one of the few French-Canadians to make good in organized baseball. He was "box office" in Montreal and everyone knew it. "Breard isn't the best player on the club," I heard Hector Racine, President of the club, say two days after practice started, "but he's the most popular with the home-town fans." Furthermore, Breard had played under Hopper the previous season and the manager liked him. You could see it in the way he treated Stan. So it was pretty obvious I'd have to play spectacular ball to win the regular shortstop job.

When we started practice, Breard, naturally, was in the first-string line-up; I was on the second team. I set out to try to make a good impression on Hopper immediately. The very first day, I was racing all over the infield, trying to make "sensational" stops and throwing as hard and fast as I could. Clyde Sukeforth told me to slow down.

75

"Don't overdo it, Jack," he said. "You're going to get a sore arm if you do."

But I refused to heed his advice. I was going to show Hopper and everyone else that I was good enough to crash that first-string infield. By the fourth day of practice, I was sure I was in mid-season condition. Hopper was hitting ground balls to us during infield practice. He hit one far to my left and I tore over to get it. I stopped the ball, picked it up, and rifled a throw to first base.

"Beautiful throw," shouted Johnny Wright from the side line.

"Nice stop," someone else hollered.

I appreciated the compliments, but not the burning, tingling pain that shot through my arm when I let the ball go. But badly as my arm ached, I didn't have sense enough to quit. I tried to hide the pain — I had to make an impression!

When I got home that evening, my arm hurt so much that I couldn't lift it to comb my hair. I rolled and tossed in bed all that night, and the next morning it was even worse. I couldn't hide my secret any longer. At practice that day, Hopper hit a ball to me and I couldn't even throw it as far as the pitcher's box — much less to first base.

So for the next three days I did nothing more than take my turn during batting practice. Hopper wouldn't even let me toss a ball on the side line. Meantime, Breard was showing his customary good form and my chances were fading fast.

On the third day, Mr. Rickey paid us a visit. He had been spending most of his time across town where the Dodgers were working out. "Listen," he said seriously, "you've got to get in there, sore arm or no sore arm. Under ordinary circumstances it would be all right, but you're not here under ordinary circumstances. You can't afford to miss a single day. They'll say you're doggin' it; that you are pretending your arm is sore."

He told Hopper to try me at second base. "He won't have to throw as far then," Mr. Rickey said. Hopper put me on second base and, believe it or not, I couldn't even throw to first from there.

When Rickey saw that, he called me over to the coaching box. "If you can't throw that far," he said, "I'll have to make a first baseman out of you." He got a first baseman's mitt and took me out on the field. He spent more than an hour showing me how to play the bag and just what to do under certain conditions.

I had never wanted to play first base. I was a shortstop and wanted to play that position, but he was the big boss and I did as he said. We played some intra-squad games for the next three days and there I was — planted right on first base, a position I was growing to detest more each day. I missed perfect throws, bobbled easily hit balls, and in general made a mighty poor excuse for a first sacker. Little did I dream that I would make my debut in the Majors at that position.

The day finally came when we were to travel across town to play the Dodgers. Everyone was keyed up for that game. "All you have to do," one of the players said, "is to make a good showing against the Dodgers and you'll be sure of staying with Montreal. They might even promote you to the Dodgers if you do well enough."

Everyone was keyed up for the Dodgers except me, that is. I didn't even know whether I'd get to play or not. Ever since I arrived in Daytona it had been rumored that the local authorities would not permit me to play against the Dodgers on their field. True, Mayor William Perry had sanctioned my training in Daytona. "No one objects to Jackie Robinson and Johnny Wright training here with Montreal," he had said in an interview. "The city officials and population simply regard them as two more

ball players. We welcome them and wish them luck." . . .
But training and playing exhibition games were two entirely different matters, it seemed. The Dodgers trained
in the heart of town, while we trained at a field located
in the center of the Negro section. No one could predict
whether or not the city officials would interfere with my
performing over in the white district. Mr. Rickey didn't
know what to expect; nor did Hopper or Mel Jones, the
business manager of the Montreal Club. "We'll just take
you and Wright along like everyone else," Mr. Rickey
said. "If there's to be an issue, we'll face it."

We went to play the Dodgers. When I walked out on
the field there were a few boos from the stands — nothing
more. The game finally got under way and Breard, the
shortstop, was the first man up. I was playing second and
batting second. When the announcer said: "Robinson,
second baseman," I expected to be showered with more
catcalls and boos. "This is where you're going to get it,"
I told myself. "This crowd does not want you here and
they're going to show it." But to my astonishment, I received a tremendous ovation. I could hear a few boos, but
they were drowned out. Above the general clamor rose a
deep, drawling Southern voice: "Come on, black boy! You
can make the grade." Then another: "They're givin' you
a chance — now come on and do somethin' about it!"
That reception made me feel mighty good inside. For the
first time in weeks I had a warm glow of hope and confidence.

Can you imagine how much I wanted to sock Ralph
Branca's fast ball high and far over the fence? . . . But I
didn't. I fouled out to the catcher. Yet as I walked back
to the bench, I still felt like a new man. I knew then that
fans — even the Southern fans — were not down on me.
Most of the people in that crowd were pulling for me. At
long last, the cloud of despondency and doubt had lifted.
I knew that from now on I could play my heart out.

I didn't get a single hit that day, nor did we win the ball game; but when I got home I felt as though I, personally, had won some kind of a victory. I had a new opinion of the people in the town. I knew, of course, that everyone wasn't pulling for me to make good, but I was sure now that the whole world wasn't lined up against me. When I went to sleep, the applause was still ringing in my ears.

I think I should say something here about Southerners. They have always been assigned the chief blame for keeping Negroes out of organized ball. Sportswriters kept asking: "What about the Southern ball players?" "How can a club go South with a Negro player on the squad?" . . . Well, I discovered that afternoon in Daytona — and many times thereafter — that most of the people below the Mason-Dixon line accepted my presence on a baseball diamond along with white players. The American sports fan — North or South — is fundamentally the same. Above everything else, he admires and respects athletic prowess, guts, and good sportsmanship. And he demands a fair chance and fair play.

From that memorable day on, I began to play better ball. I started hitting and my fielding improved. My arm even got better and I rapidly gained confidence. Of course, I ran into racial problems on other occasions, but I always consoled myself with the memory of Daytona Beach.

One of those occasions occurred a short time afterward. We were scheduled to play an exhibition game with the Jersey City Giants in Jacksonville. We made the trip by bus, and when we arrived at the park there was a big crowd waiting outside. We climbed out and went over to the players' gate leading onto the field. It was locked. We couldn't get in; nor, apparently, could the waiting fans.

"What's wrong here?" Hopper asked a man standing near-by.

"The game's been called off," the man said. "The Bureau of Recreation won't let the game be played because you've got colored guys on your club."

Mel Jones got hold of Charley Stoneham, the Jersey City business manager, and found that the man's report was correct. George Robinson, executive secretary of the Bureau of Recreation, had informed the Jersey City club that he would not allow the game to be played. There was nothing for us to do but drive back to Daytona.

Johnny Wright and I were pretty unhappy. We felt responsible for all the trouble. But we did have one consolation: a big crowd had been waiting to see the game. They were standing in long lines when we arrived. That meant a lot to us. It meant that it wasn't the people of Jacksonville who objected to our playing in their park — it was the politicians. Had the decision been left to all those people in line, the game would have been played.

We got back to Daytona in time to play a game anyway. We drove right to the Dodgers' Park. They were practicing and Hopper and Leo Durocher decided to have a game. It seemed to me that our gang took its feelings out on the Big Leaguers that day. Anyway, we beat them five to three.

At Deland, Florida about a week later, we were scheduled to play an exhibition game there with Indianapolis. It had been rumored that I would not be permitted to play, but Mr. Rickey insisted that Johnny Wright and I go along.

I took batting and infield practice with the team and no one made any objections. It looked as though the rumors had been false, and so Hopper started me at second base. We were the visiting team and consequently batted first. I was up second and got a base hit. I stole second and the next hitter, Tom Tatum, singled to left

had just signed my first contract to play in the Big Leagues. It was a great moment, not only for me, but for my race.

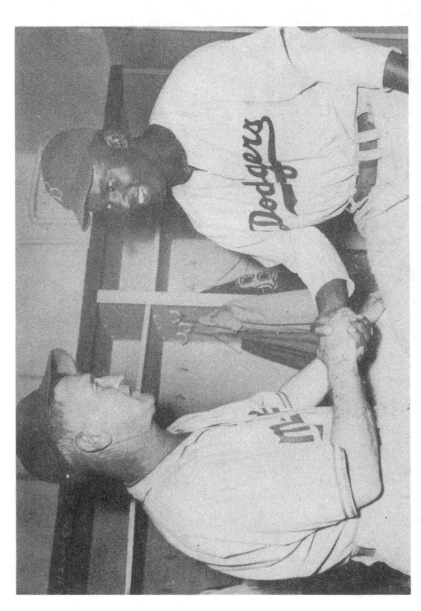

I really enjoyed playing under Clay Hopper, my manager at Montreal. When I left his team he said, "Jackie, you are a real ball-player and a gentleman." Hopper, off season, has a cotton plantation in Mississippi.

It was Clyde Sukeforth who discovered me while I was playing with the Kansas City Monarchs. Here he is shaking hands with me. On the left is Ray Blades, and on the right is Jake Pitler, both Dodger coaches. It was Sukeforth who was always coming to my rescue when I was about to lose my temper.

I had started as a shortstop for the Kansas City Monarchs, played second base for the Montreal Royals, and switched to first base for the Dodgers although I disliked playing the initial sack at the beginning. Here, in an exhibition game with the Yankees, I was just learning to play the position. It wasn't until later on in 1947 that I really felt at home at first base.

Learning to play first base and trying to break into the Big Leagues at the same time was probably the biggest problem of my career. I had never before, even in kid games, played first base. I never thought I'd be successful.

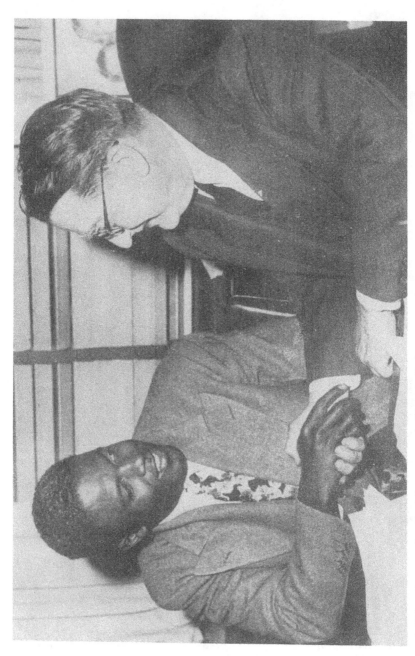

Branch Rickey is more than just the owner of a baseball club. To me he has been like the father I never knew, advising and helping me over all the rough spots, and there have been plenty of them.

"Let them know you're on the base path," Branch Rickey told me at the start of my career with the Dodger organization. I tried to follow his advice by worrying the pitchers, dancing up and down, and attempting to steal as often as I could. Here I've just stolen second against the Yankees in the first game of the 1947 World Series.

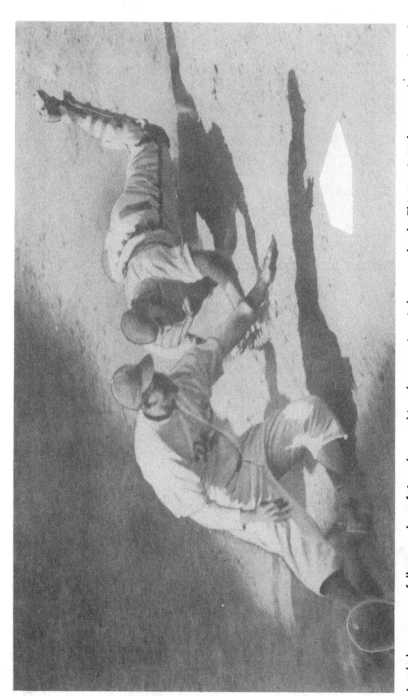

I stole home successfully a number of times by watching the opposing pitcher very closely. This time I tried to score from second on a single, but because I overslid the plate, the catcher tagged me out. Branch Rickey told me Ty Cobb wasn't always successful either.

After Leo Durocher was suspended, Burt Shotten managed the Dodgers for the season of 1947. He was always kind and helpful to me and a great man to work for.

The umpire is all set to give his decision on this very close play. Phil Rizzuto of the Yankees beat the throw by an eyelash.

One of the great thrills in baseball is smacking one on the nose and lining it down the base line.

I had some practice playing against the Yankees before the 1947 World Series. In this exhibition game in April 1947, Billy Johnson, Yankee third baseman, tagged me out as I slid into the bag.

In a crucial Cub-Dodger series in Chicago, Johnny Schmitz, Cub pitcher, made a wild pitch and I chased down to second, just beating the throw to shortstop Len Merullo. We won this game, 4 to 0.

In the opening game of a late-season series with the Cardinals in St. Louis, I caught hold of a fast one and socked it for a two-run homer. Eddie Stanky, my second base neighbor and pal, was waiting at home plate to shake my hand.

Before game time I usually have a session with the kids at Ebbets Field, signing their score cards. It's a great thrill for me to talk to the youngsters.

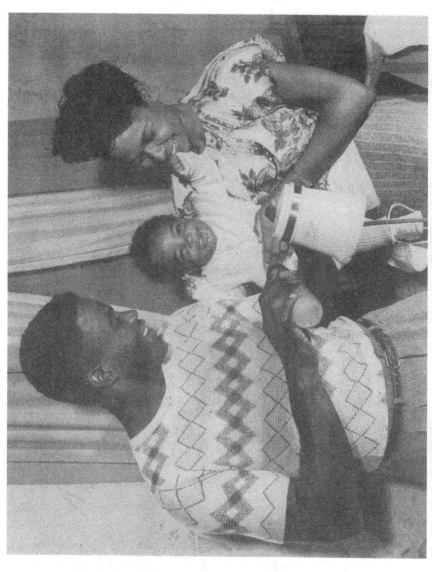

My wife, Rachel, gave birth to a bouncing baby boy whom we named Jackie, Jr. We vowed to give him all the things we had missed as kids. I hope he will be a great athlete, and I don't think he will have as many barriers to break through as I had.

center. I took off for third base and Hopper, who was in the coaching box, waved me on home. I rounded the bag under full steam and headed for the plate. I knew it was going to be close and that I'd have to slide to make it. I took a big breath and left my feet, sliding across just ahead of the throw. The stands were cheering and I felt good. We were one run ahead and it was still the first inning. But before I could get up and head for the bench, a strong firm hand appeared through the cloud of dust I had raised and grasped me by the collar. At first I thought the next batter on my team was trying to help me up, and I was about to thank him. But just then the dust cleared away and I recognized the standard uniform of the Law.

"Now you git off'n this heah field right now," he drawled. "Eff'n ya don't, ah'm puttin' ya' in the jail house right now. So hep me eff ah don't!"

At first I was tempted to laugh, but I could see he was dead serious. I suddenly saw myself behind bars wearing a baseball uniform. . . . By this time the crowd in the stands was on its feet. The Indianapolis ball players didn't move. They just stayed at their positions, waiting to see what was going to happen. The policeman finally released his death-grip on my collar and I sauntered toward the bench. Hopper, obviously flustered, made a belated and reluctant appearance from the dugout. "What's wrong?" he asked in a voice as typically Southern as the policeman's. "He didn't do anything wrong, did he?"

"Yes, he did," the cop snapped back.

"What?" Hopper asked meekly.

"We told y'all to leave them Nigra players home," said Deland's legal guardian. "We ain't having Nigras and white boys playing on the same field in this town. It's agin the law and ah'm heah to tell ya."

Hopper turned to see if I had gone to the dressing room. I hadn't. I was sitting on the bench with the rest of the

97

team, watching the show. The cop was looking at me, too. He had a scowl on his sun-tanned countenance; certainly he wasn't in a jovial mood.

"Y'all ain't up-states now," the policeman informed Hopper. "Ya can't come down heah and change our way of livin'. They's a law says Nigras and whites cain't be togetha. They cain't sit togetha; and ya' know damn well they cain't git married togetha!"

I felt sorry for Hopper. He didn't know what to do. He knew he had to do what the cop said, but he didn't want to have to tell me to leave the game. I knew then he was beginning to like me.

"Git him off'en thet there bench," the cop demanded, waving his menacing-looking club. "He cain't set there. They's white boys a-setin' there. Thet's agin the law, too. They cain't set togetha on no baseball benches, either."

By now the crowd was shouting for the game to continue. The players were getting restless and so was the cop. In order to relieve Hopper the embarrassment of having to tell me to leave, I decided to do it voluntarily.

Hopper started walking toward the bench. I guess he had decided he'd have to tell me, although I could see he didn't want to.

The cop was walking a few feet behind him, waving his stick and getting more boisterous. "Tell him ah said to git!" the cop bellowed.

Hopper was within a few feet of me now. He took a deep breath and said, "Jackie — ah — the cop says — "

But before he could say any more I threw up my hand to save him the embarrassment. "Okay, Skipper," I said, using my best imitation of a Southern drawl, "tell him that ah'm a-gittin'."

And I headed for the shower room with Johnny Wright on my heels.

International Merry-Go-Round

THE BIRDS WERE BEGINNING TO WING THEIR WAY NORTH now, and we were ready to start the long pennant grind in the International League. On April 14, we packed our bags, said good-by to Daytona Beach, and headed for Jersey City and opening day.

There was considerable fanfare and excitement at Roosevelt Stadium on opening day in 1946. Approximately 35,000 fans turned out. There was no school that day and the kids came en masse. Mayor Frank Hague was there, too. He led the parade of dignitaries and players to the flag pole. They unfurled Old Glory and we sang "The Star Spangled Banner." I guess the anthem meant more to me that day than ever before. Johnny Wright was standing beside me. There was a lump in my throat as the band blared out and we all sang the familiar words.

It was a beautiful day. The sun shone down on the big American flag as it climbed up the pole, and the air had the crisp freshness of an October day. It was ideal football weather, and indeed the crowd looked and acted more like a football crowd than a baseball crowd. The kids were waving pennants and shouting and yelping all over the big stadium. Men were wearing light topcoats and the vendors were selling hot, steaming coffee. Few people were buying ice cream.

The public address system boomed out the starting line-ups, and the groundkeepers dressed the field with im-

99

maculate white foul lines to right and left field. As the game approached, it seemed to me that everyone present felt some of the same mounting tension I did. This was more than the mere excitement of an opening day. We all sensed that history was in the making — that the long ban against Negro players was about to come crashing down, setting up reverberations that would echo across a continent and perhaps around the world. I believe everyone in Roosevelt Stadium that day realized that he was witnessing a significant collapse in the ancient wall of prejudice.

Certainly it was an exciting moment in my life. I was about to enter organized baseball. I had always longed to play Big League ball, and here I was with an honest-to-goodness chance. I knew within me that I was going to make good — I *had* to make good! I never doubted that if I played well in this league, someday I'd move across the river. It wasn't so far now to the Majors. All you had to do was go through the Hudson Tunnel, cross the big bridge from Manhattan, and put your feet down in Brooklyn — that is, if you took the short route! No, it wasn't far geographically, but it was at least 150 games and 12 long months away. And my route would be rough and hazardous and perhaps lonely. . . .

Just before game time, Hopper took us into the dressing room for a pep talk. We all sat down in a semicircle. "Now let's get off to a flying start," he said. "Pennants are won in the first weeks of the season. Let's get this one over with and then pile up such a big lead no one will be able to catch us." He then announced the starting line-up and I was at second base. We went back out on the field. The umpire shouted: "Play ball!" There was a deafening roar as the Jersey City Giants ran out on the field in their spic and span new uniforms.

Shortstop Stan Breard was the first batter. He went out, short to first. I was up next. Although I was wearing the colors of the enemy, the Jersey City fans gave me a fine ovation; and my teammates were shouting, "Come on, Jackie, start it off. This guy can't pitch. Get a-hold of one!" They couldn't have wanted me to get a hit half as much as I wanted to.

I worked the count to three and two and then hit an easy bounder to the shortstop. He threw me out by four or five steps.

I came up again in the second inning. This time I got my first hit in organized baseball. Tom Tatum and George Shuba were on base and we were leading by one run. Once again I worked the count to three and two. I swung the next pitch with everything I had. There was a crack like a rifle shot in my ears. The ball sailed some 340 feet and disappeared over the left-field fence. Tatum and Shuba trotted home ahead of me. Once again those Jersey City fans cheered and applauded, and when I crossed home plate, George Shuba was waiting for me. "That's the way to hit that ball, Jackie," Shuba said. "That's the old ball game right there." He shook my hand.

"That's the way to hit 'em," Marvin Rackley said when I sat down beside him on the bench. Rackley was a brilliant outfielder from South Carolina. "Nice going, Jackie," said third baseman Johnny Jorgenson. I felt happy little butterflies fluttering around in my stomach.

When I came up in the fifth inning, I sort of sensed that they were expecting me to swing away again. I decided to try to cross them up. So I bunted down the third-base line and caught them flat-footed.

On the second pitch to the next batter, I tore out for second and made it safely. Tom Tatum then hit a hot one to third. Jersey's Larry Niggins made a fine stop on the play and whipped the ball over to first. As he made the throw, I took off for third. Tom was out, but I managed to beat Norm Jaeger's throw from first back to third by an eyelash.

As I dusted myself off, I remembered one morning down in Daytona Beach when Mr. Rickey had called me and said he wanted to talk to me. I went to see him. "Jackie," he said, "I want you to run the bases like blazes. I want you to worry the pitchers so much they won't know what to do. Steal all the bases you can. Sometimes, of course, they'll catch you. But don't worry about that. The best base runners get caught. Ty Cobb got caught plenty. I'm going to let you run the bases just as you see fit. Don't be reckless. Just be smart and cagey, and when you think you can make it — run like the devil!"

Standing on third base in my first League game, I recalled that advice. I'd try to steal home. Phil Oates was pitching for Jersey City. When he got ready to pitch, he took a windup and I ran more than halfway down the base path. I might have gone all the way that time, but I decided not to. When Oates got ready to pitch again, I took a big lead off third. He tried to catch me off, but I slid back safely. "I got him worried now," I said to myself. "I think I'll try to go all the way this time." So when Phil took his windup, I put my head down and ran like the devil. Oates got so rattled that he failed to complete his windup. It was a balk. The umpire threw up his hands and waved me on home.

In the seventh I singled for my third straight hit and stole second again. Tom Tatum singled me home and I scored for the third time that day. In the eighth I socked a single to left. I finally got as far as third base and once again started dancing menacingly up and down the base line. Herb Andrews was pitching for Jersey City now and he also got flustered and committed a balk. Once again the umpire waved me home.

Needless to say, we won that opening game. The final score was 14 to 1. And I had had a lucky day — four hits in five trips to the plate, including a home run; four runs batted in; two stolen bases; and four runs scored, two of them by making Jersey City pitchers balk. In the field, I had made one error when I pivoted wrong on a double-play ball hit by Cleston Ray to Jorgensen at third; but I had handled six chances and in the sixth inning had started our only double play of the day.

After the game the crowd just about mobbed me. Kids were chasing me all over the place to get my autograph and grown people were patting me on the back. The significant thing was that they were all Jersey City fans. Once again I was convinced that American sports fans are truly democratic. I was sure now that they would accept me — that they didn't care what color a player was. All I had to do was play good ball and never stop trying. And I knew, too, that if the fans like you, the chances of your making good are much better than if they are down on you.

I was a very happy guy that night when I returned to my hotel. My wife was happy, too. "You were wonderful today," she said when we got to the hotel. "I was so thrilled!"

"You weren't any more thrilled than I was," I told her. "I was just plain lucky. God must have smiled on me today."

The following day the papers gave me some fine write-ups. International News Service, United Press, Associated Press, and most of the New York and Montreal papers had sent men to cover this "historic opener." I was off to a flying start. Could I keep going? That was the big question.

We took the series from Jersey City, then moved to Newark and on to Syracuse. Our last series on the road was with Baltimore. After that we headed for Montreal and the home opener.

We flew from Baltimore in two big transport planes.

Jackie Robinson

The day was bleak and cold. When the plane I was in hit the runway at the Montreal airport, I was wondering just how the people there would react to my presence on the team. I wondered if they'd like me. What did the future hold in store for me here in this quiet, conservative Canadian city? ...

We beat Jersey City in our opener at home two days later and then took stock of our pennant chances. We had seen all the clubs in the League and we knew we were in for a long, hard fight. There was plenty of competition. Baltimore, Syracuse, and Newark had sound, strong ball clubs. We knew then that they would be our main rivals. We'd have to play first-class ball.

I knew that it was going to be exceptionally tough for me. Not only did I have to play good ball, but I also had to be prepared to take anything the other teams and the fans would dish out to me. Every ball player has to take his share of riding and jockeying, but most can give as well as take. And rarely is he made the butt of insults and obscene vilification because of his race or nationality. After all, he can use his fists. But I couldn't. I had to keep my mouth shut and my hands at my sides no matter what.

I liked Montreal immediately. I liked it because it seemed to like me. The people were friendly and gracious. The kids on the street made a fuss over me and the adults smiled and shook my hand wherever I went. The city is composed in the main of French-Canadians, and consequently the announcers at the park make all announcements in both French and English. The first few days they intrigued me. When they announced my name in French over the public address system it sounded like *Yakee Rob-een-son.* I used to say to myself: "That doesn't sound like your name, but it is." I liked it. Why, I don't know. Maybe it was because I was very happy there. Maybe it was because I was an escapist at heart and when they said my name in French, I imagined I wasn't Jackie Robinson at all. I wasn't the player of whom so many things were expected. I was Yakee Rob-een-son, the new second baseman of the Montreal Royals.

Well, we got off to a flying start at the very beginning of the season. On the first of August, we were something like fifteen games in front. By August 28, we had clinched the pennant and were looking forward to the play-offs which determine the International League representative in the Little World Series.

I was having a good year. Luck was with me. I was socking the ball at a .360 clip, fielding well at second base, and runner-up to my teammate Marvin Rackley for base stealing honors. But all through the season I had been under terrific strain. I wanted to help win the pennant and also the batting championship. When we sewed up the flag, I suddenly felt completely exhausted. My average began to slip. I was listless, nervous, and irritable. The letdown became so obvious that both my wife and Clay Hopper insisted that I consult a doctor. I finally agreed and went to see one. "You've been under too much tension," he said. "I want you to get away from baseball and rest for ten days. I don't want you even to think about it. Don't read the newspapers or listen to the radio. Do something you enjoy, something that will relax you. Your nerves are about to explode." He advised me to play golf because I told him that was my favorite hobby.

So I left the team and took it easy for four days. Then I rejoined the club and finished out the season. My luck held and I won the batting championship with an average of .349; I was second in base stealing with forty (Marvin Rackley won honors in that department with sixty thefts) ; I tied Clarence "Soup" Campbell of Baltimore for most runs scored, with 113; and I had the best second-base fielding percentage in the League.

The entire season in the International League had been an enjoyable one. I ran into a few problems, but they solved themselves. Syracuse rode me harder than any other city in the circuit. They were tough on me both on the field and in the stands. One time, for instance, as I came up to bat during a game there, one of the Syracuse players came out of the dugout holding a black cat. "Hey, Robinson," he shouted, "here's one of your relatives!"

The other players on the bench laughed. I was sore all right, but sometimes anger is a spur to an athlete. I was going to hit that ball hard if it was the last thing I ever did! . . .

Well, I smacked it for a double — about the most satisfactory one I ever hit in my life. A few moments later a base hit sent me home with the winning run. As I rounded third, I yelled to the players on the Syracuse bench: "I guess that relative of mine is happy now, isn't he?" If there was any answer, I didn't hear it.

Some people, including the President of the International League, had anticipated trouble for me in Baltimore, but I never encountered trouble there. The first time I played in Baltimore, there was some ugly name-calling; but as the season went on, Baltimore players and fans treated me well. One night I stole home in a close game and the Baltimore fans gave me a great ovation.

As the season drew near its close, Brooklyn was in a death struggle with the St. Louis Cardinals for the National League pennant. They were going down the stretch neck-and-neck. There was considerable speculation in the papers as to whether or not Brooklyn would call me up to help out in the race. Some writers thought Brooklyn might use me in this final drive. They predicted that I'd be called up from Montreal.

Mr. Rickey, however, put a stop to the talk. He announced that I would remain with Montreal. "The

Royals are in a play-off," he pointed out. "Robinson is the property of that club and will stay there. We owe it to the Montreal fans to keep him there. They want to see their team in the Little World Series just as badly as the Brooklyn fans want to see the Dodgers in the big World Series."

So I stayed at Montreal and we went on to win the play-offs and the right to meet Louisville, winners of the American Association race, in the Little World Series.

In Louisville, the fans were still race-conscious. There were no Negro players in the Association, and a lot of the white rooters obviously resented my presence in their ball park. Whenever I came to bat, they gave me the works. Not all of them, understand, but most of them. To make matters worse, my hitting was pitiful. My combined batting average for those three games was under .200. I was still tired from the strain of the long season that lay behind. I guess some of the fans booed me because I didn't live up to expectations.

We lost two out of three games to Louisville and went back to Montreal on the short end. However, we found ourselves in our home park and won the next three games. I was much happier playing in Montreal and my playing became an asset to the club. I averaged .400 at the plate and scored the winning run in the final game that gave us the title of "Little World Champions."

I'll never forget the demonstration that followed that final game. The papers said the next day that it had never been equaled in the history of Minor League baseball. Certainly I never experienced anything like it before, and probably never will again.

Right after that last game I had to catch a plane. I dashed into the dressing room and amid all the shouting and cheering tried to dress in a hurry. Meantime, thousands of people were still in the park, shouting and cheering. The police and ushers were begging them to leave the park, but they refused to go.

Sam Maltin told the story in the *Pittsburgh Courier*: "Ushers and police couldn't keep the crowd from the field. They refused to move and sang 'Il a gagne ses Epaulettes' (He won his bars) and 'We want Robinson.' It was a mob ready to riot. Manager Clay Hopper came out of the clubhouse and they chaired him on their shoulders and carried him around the field. Then veteran pitcher Curt Davis, who hurled the final victory, made his appearance and they carted him around. But there was no Robinson and they refused to move until he showed himself.

"A delegation of ushers went to see Jackie and asked him to step out, so that they could close the park and call it a season. Jackie came out and the crowd surged on him. Men and women of all ages threw their arms around him, kissed him, pulled and tore at his clothes, and then carried him around the infield on their shoulders, shouting themselves hoarse.

"Jackie, tears streaming down his face, tried to beg off further honors.

"They carried him back to the clubhouse. There, he had a tough time packing his gear as people came trooping in to wish him luck. They all said they wanted him back.

"All through this, little Frenchy, the Montreal mascot, stood close to Jackie listening to his well-wishers; and then he piped up with: 'Jackie, I never want to see you here again!'

"Jackie understood. He put his arms around the kid, smiled, and said: 'Thanks, French. Thanks very much!' "

I was the last to leave the dressing room. Before Manager Hopper left, he came to me and shook my hand. "Jackie," he said, "you're a real ball player and a gentleman. It's been wonderful having you on the team."

"Thanks, Skipper," I said. "It's been wonderful playing under you."

Hopper was on his way back to Mississippi and his cotton plantation.

All the other players shook my hand and said good-by.

"I'm glad you were on this club," Marvin Rackley said. "You're a fine guy, Jackie. I hope you make the Majors next season." He was on his way to his home in Walhalla, South Carolina.

When I at last got ready to leave the dressing room, the passageway was blocked with at least three hundred people. Every time I opened the door, they'd start yelling and pushing. I couldn't get out, and the ushers and police couldn't break through and come to my rescue. Finally, I had to take a chance. I passed my bag to a friend, hunched my shoulders, and plunged smack into that throng. Here's how Sam Maltin described it in his story:

"It was a demonstration seldom seen here. Again the crowd started hugging and kissing him. He tried to explain that he had to catch a plane. They wouldn't listen, refused to hear him.

"They held on to him, but — as he had done in his football days at UCLA — Robbie gently fought off his admirers and pushed his way through until he found an opening. Then he started running.

"The mob was running after him. Down the street he went, chased by five hundred fans. People opened windows and came pouring out of their houses to see what the commotion was about. For three blocks they chased him until a car drew up and someone shouted: 'Jump in, Jackie!' That he did, and sat down — plunk in a lady's lap. They brought him safely to the hotel.

"Men three times the age of Robinson, oldtimers in the local sports scene, men who had seen some of the greatest Canadian athletes in action, failed to recall an ovation that matched that given to Robinson.

"It wasn't an organized reception; it was as spontaneous as the booing aimed at every Louisville player that had stepped up to the plate in Montreal — an answer to the jeering given Jackie in the Kentucky city during the first three games.

"To the large group of Louisville fans who came here with their team, it may be a lesson of good will among men. They may have learned that it's the man — not his color, race, or creed.

"They couldn't fail to tell others down South of the riot, the chasing of a Negro — not because of hate but because of love!"

As my plane roared skyward and the lights of Montreal twinkled and winked in the distance, I took one last look at this great city where I had found so much happiness.

"I don't care if I never get to the Majors," I told myself. "This is the city for me. This is paradise."

"Trouble-Maker"

IN JANUARY OF 1947 THE ASSOCIATED PRESS POLLED SPORTS editors across the country to find out what they considered the No. 1 sports question for the ensuing year. They voted that the No. 1 question was whether or not I would become the first Negro player to make the grade in Big League baseball. I can assure you it was the No. 1 question in my mind at that time, too.

I believed I had the natural ability, but would I be able to hit anywhere near what I hit the previous year at Montreal, or would the pressure give me the jitters? This was just one of the many questions in my mind as the time drew near for me to go to Havana for spring training.

I kept telling myself: "The good Lord was on your side last year at Montreal — just pray He'll be on your side this year when you try out for the Dodgers."

I must admit that on the night I was to leave my wife and family for Havana, I was so nervous and upset that I didn't want to go. I went out to the airport to get the plane for Miami. My wife was with me. She kept talking to me on the way and I listened to every word she said. She told me just to be Jackie Robinson, to act as though I were still an athlete in college, and to assume that I could do just as well as I had done at UCLA. I tried to believe her, but I knew the days ahead were going to be the toughest of my life so far. I had to make good not only for Jackie Robinson, but also for her, for my little

111

son, and for the millions of my race across the country who were counting on me. I knew that if I failed, people who were opposed to the move — people who objected to Negroes' breaking into organized baseball — would say: "See there, didn't I tell you the white players and fans would never stand for it? They ought to stay in their places."

The one thing my wife kept cautioning me about was my temper. I had the reputation on the West Coast of being an athlete with a quick temper. They said I had a habit of flaring up and fighting back if necessary. Usually that is regarded as a good trait in an athlete. It means that the fellow is a fighter and game to the core. College coaches like men like that. I think I did fight to win as hard as the other boys on our UCLA teams and on the other teams we played, but I don't think I was ever a "sore-head" or a trouble-maker. Many things of which I had been accused were simply untrue.

I knew, however, that I would have to live down my reputation — no matter how unjustified — from the moment I arrived in training camp. Because I was a Negro, I knew I had to remain calm all the time. My wife also knew it, and she kept drilling the admonition into my mind. I guess she half-believed I was hotheaded, because she had been present several times when I had encountered discrimination and had seen me get so angry that I had almost blown up. These occasions had produced whispers: "That Jackie Robinson may be a good athlete, but he has a bad temper." The whispers were so consistent and far-flung that they had reached Brooklyn. I learned, in fact, that Branch Rickey was more than a little concerned over this alleged characteristic of mine. He had said that he was going to try to "harness" me, but that if he couldn't, he would give me my release. That made me realize what a great risk he had taken in signing me. If I didn't keep my temper, I would embarrass not only him, but thousands of other people who were pulling for me to make good.

On the way to the airport, I listened to my wife. I made up my mind that I was going to disprove that "bad temper" propaganda. The rumor had begun when I was in college. In the heat of games, any athlete will scream "murder" sometimes, and I was no exception. If a UCLA player got roughed-up in a football game, for instance, I was right in the middle of any ruckus that developed. Maybe I was a bit too aggressive in those days. After all, I was a Negro, and the pattern of conduct for Negroes in almost any relation with white people has been, if not a subservient attitude, at least one of keeping quiet and remaining in the background. I don't think I was more aggressive than the other players, but I guess people were just not used to seeing a Negro heatedly "talking back" to white men in the very middle of a stadium jammed with thousands of people.

However, the one incident above all others that had convinced some people that I was a "tough" happened far from any athletic field. It happened in 1938. With some of my friends, I was driving home from a softball game. We bumped into a white man's car in front of us. An argument ensued, a crowd gathered, and the police came. Instead of trying to settle the argument and fairly establish who was at fault, the police decided we were some young colored fellows ·wanted for committing a robbery. They took us to the police station and booked us. The story got into the papers and when people saw my name, I guess they said: "I'm not surprised. I knew he'd get into trouble some day."

Anyway, I had to appeal to my friends. Coach Harrell of UCLA and some other influential people came to my aid. They assured the police that I wasn't one of the fellows they were looking for, and subsequently I was re-

113

leased. I had to forfeit twenty-five dollars' bond, however, before they would let me go.

Although I was entirely innocent, that incident established me as a trouble-maker. Later on, all through school, I kept hearing rumors that I was causing dissension on the team. These were picked up by the press. I knew they weren't true; so did my coaches. But there wasn't anything I could do. I just kept quiet and hoped the gossip would die out.

After my college days, I thought I had lived down that reputation. But as soon as I was assigned to the Montreal Club, it came popping up again — so prominently that Branch Rickey heard it. . . . I was just plain discouraged.

As we drove out to the Los Angeles airport on that February night in 1947, all these things were running through my head. My wife told me good-by at the airport and went home. I went inside to purchase my ticket. "The plane to Miami has been grounded and won't leave until some time tomorrow," the ticket clerk said. Under ordinary circumstances, I would have been disappointed, but I was glad — very glad. I suddenly didn't want to leave my wife and son; I wanted to be near my mother. Cheerfully I grabbed a taxi and headed for home.

When I walked into the house, my wife's eyes popped wide open. "What in the world are you doing back here? I thought you were on the way to Havana," she said.

I smiled and shrugged my shoulders. "The planes aren't flying," I informed her gleefully. "They won't take off until sometime tomorrow. Aren't you glad?"

"No," she said firmly and emphatically. "I don't like this. I don't like to see things start off like this; I want you to be there on time. You know the first impression is everlasting. I hate to see you leave, but after all, there is more involved in this than Jackie and Rachel Robinson."

I tried to soothe her. "Look," I explained, "Manager Clay Hopper will give me a day or two grace. It isn't as if I were going to report to Brooklyn. I'm reporting to Montreal and I think they like me enough to grant me a few extra days."

My wife didn't like that attitude. "You're going to report to Montreal," she said, "but that's because Mr. Rickey wants it that way. You know as well as I do that he wants everything to work out right. Montreal is just a veil as far as you're concerned. You are going to be a Dodger in April. You shouldn't do anything that will put a block in Mr. Rickey's path."

I listened to her and had to agree she was right. I hadn't given much thought to Mr. Rickey's problem — just to my own. When she put it the way she did, I realized I had been unconsciously dreading to face my big test. And she was absolutely right about our not being the only ones involved in this. Aftter all, Rachel was my wife. We would always stick by each other, no matter what. We had decided that when we were school kids, and I never questioned it for a moment. But there was Jackie, Jr. . . . Well, he's my son; he will always understand, I told myself. But on second thought, I wondered. . . . What would he say in years to come when kids on the street would ask: "Say, whatever happened to your dad? They tell us at home that he had a chance to become the first Negro player in the Big Leagues and that he muffed the chance because he reported to training camp late. Thought he was such a hot-shot that he could get away with it."

The next day I was up bright and early, ready to go. I felt like a man about to leave for the battle front. The job was before me and I just had to do it. When I thought about what my wife had said the night before,

I realized that without her I might have turned out to be "baseball's No. 1 flop."

By the time I had to leave for the airport, I was set and ready for the journey that would make me or break me. The skies were clear; the sun shone down with a pleasant warmth. The planes were flying and Havana lay thousands of miles ahead. . . . I kissed my wonderful wife and son good-by.

When I climbed aboard the plane the hostess said, "Name please?"

"Jackie Robinson," I said.

"Oh," she said, raising her eyebrows, "you're going to join the Brooklyn Dodgers, aren't you?"

I gave her my ticket and said, "I sure am, lady, come hell or high water."

Soon after, the big plane roared down the run-way and took off. I was on my way to Havana — and the Brooklyn Dodgers.

*C*an I Fill That Gap?

WOULD I PLAY WITH THE BROOKLYN DODGERS? NOBODY seemed to know. Not even Mr. Rickey. When newspapermen asked him if I would be promoted to the Big League club, he said: "That remains to be seen. Right now, he is still a member of the Montreal Club. He will go to spring training with that team. What develops after that, I can't say. It all depends on the circumstances."

Montreal and the Dodgers were both training in Havana. Three other Negro players were on the Montreal squad: Roy Campanella, a catcher (and a close friend of mine); and Don Newcombe and Roy Partlow, both pitchers. Campanella and Newcombe had played with the Dodgers' Nashua Club in the New England League the previous year, while Partlow, a veteran, had played with Montreal and Three Rivers (Quebec), the latter a Dodger farm club in the Canadian American League.

When I arrived at camp, I was greeted by Hopper and the fellows I had played with the previous year. Only this time it was an enthusiastic, joyous meeting. The year before, when I was making my bid in Florida, there had been no such hospitality or friendliness, and I had been tense and ill at ease. I had had to adjust myself to a situation in which many people were hostile. Now it was entirely different. I was welcome — an accepted member of the club.

There were two members of our 1946 championship

team missing. Marvin Rackley and Tom Tatum had been called up by Brooklyn and were in the Dodgers' camp in Havana proper. We trained at the Havana Military Academy, fifteen miles away. I found myself wishing I had been as lucky as Tatum and Rackley.

We went through four days of conditioning, running around the field and taking setting-up exercises. When the drills were over, the other players retired to the school dormitory. We four Negro players had to go to a hotel in Havana. That meant we traveled thirty miles every day. We didn't know why we weren't accommodated in the dormitory with the other players. I had stayed in the same hotels with the rest of the team the year before and, so far as I know, none of them had ever objected. Yet here was the old Jim Crow pattern down in Cuba, a democracy made up chiefly of "colored" peoples.

Later on, we discovered that Mr. Rickey, moving with extreme care, had decided it would be best for us to live that way. He felt that there might be some new players on the Montreal squad who would resent sharing living quarters with us. "I can't afford to let anything happen," he told us. "I want this training session to be smooth. I can't afford to have any 'incidents.'"

So we went to the hotel. I didn't like it, but I decided it would be foolish to endanger my big opportunity by putting up a squawk over where I was going to sleep. A big furor might make Rickey decide it would be against the best interests of the Dodgers to sign me.

We played all our games at the Havana Stadium. The first two weeks we played against the Dodgers "B" team, composed for the most part of players who were prospects and likely to be farmed out. We also played against the Havana All-Stars, a Cuban team made up of players from the "Winter League." Most of the games were at night and we did very well. Campanella and I were hitting the ball hard, but Newcombe and Partlow were having some trouble with their control; in fact, they were having difficulty staying in the box for more than a few innings.

Finally the time came for us to go to Panama. We were scheduled to play the Dodgers a series of games there. This series was vitally important to me. For one thing, it would be a test of what I could do against Big-League pitching; but more crucial still, was my debut at first base.

One day Mel Jones, Montreal business manager, had come to me and said, "Jackie, here's a first baseman's mitt. Mr. Rickey said for you to play first base from now on."

I looked at him in amazement. Except for that time in Florida when I first joined the Montreal club and had been anchored to first because of a lame arm, I had never played first base in my life. I had hated the position then; and now, of all times, I didn't want to be shifted from a position I could play to one that I knew literally nothing about. I say now, of all times, because I wasn't feeling any too well. I was having trouble with my stomach and my back, and had a bad toe on my right foot. I had been to the doctor for all three ailments, and the results were far from gratifying. First base is a busy place. You have to do a lot of running, stretching, bending, and throwing. At second base you get a little chance to rest.

"Listen," I grumbled to Mel Jones, "I want to play second base. Gee, that's my position. Didn't I do all right there last year?"

Mel shrugged his shoulders and said, "I'm sorry, Jack, but I'm just passing down an order to you from the boss. He wants you on first base."

I took the glove and started trying to play first base in practice. I was terrible. Not only did I not know anything about the position, but I was not anxious to learn. So when we arrived in Panama to meet the Dodgers, I was a disgruntled ball player.

On the day we were to play our first game against the

119

Dodgers, Mr. Rickey called and said he wanted to see me at his hotel. I went over. "Jackie," he said, "this is the most important part of your baseball career. Nothing you did last year at Montreal means a thing. This is where you will have to make the grade. I want you to be a whirling demon against the Dodgers in this series. You have to be so good that the Dodger players themselves are going to want you on their club. After all, these boys are thinking about winning the National League Pennant.

"We are definitely weak at first base and they all know it. I believe if you show them you're the man who can fill that gap, they won't object to having you.

"I want you to hit that ball," he said. "I want you to get on base and run wild. Steal their pants off. Be the most conspicuous player on the field. The newspapermen from New York will send good stories back about you and help mold favorable public opinion."

We played seven games with the Dodgers in Panama. I probably wasn't as sensational as Mr. Rickey wanted me to be, but I certainly wasn't out of sight. I led both clubs in hitting with a mark of .625, fielded fairly well at first, and stole seven bases. And I was happy because I thought I must have demonstrated to the Brooklyn regulars that I could "fill that gap."

Soon after, I found that some Dodgers were impressed and other were not. Those who just couldn't be convinced expressed their views openly and suggested an organized move to keep me off the club. This, however, was quickly squelched. From what I gathered later, the leaders were players who had big question marks on their own uniforms. They weren't the established regulars.

After that series we flew back to Cuba. We were to wind up our training there and head for New York in ten days. One evening I was sitting in my room reading when Wendell Smith came in. I could tell he was bubbling over with news. "I just left Mr. Rickey's hotel room," he blurted. "He told me he's going to put you on the Dodgers on April 10."

I laughed at him. "If Mr. Rickey was going to put me on the Dodgers, he'd have put me on the club by now," I said. "Why would he wait until two days before the season opened? Didn't I prove down in Panama that I could hit Big League pitching and steal against Big League catchers?"

We didn't discuss it any further. Roy Campanella came in and we started a game of pinochle. Every time I thought about what Smith had said, I grunted.

"What's the matter with him?" Roy asked Smith.

"He's got indigestion again," Smith said.

We arrived in New York on April 8 and were scheduled to play the Dodgers exhibition games the two following days. And April 10 did come at last, though I had thought it never would. The baseball world was sizzling that day. Commissioner Chandler had suspended Leo Durocher for one year and the big question was: Who is going to manage the Dodgers? The papers were full of the Durocher case, and out at Ebbets Field the Brooklyn fans were carrying big signs that read: "We want our Leo back!" The suspension had created such a sensation that the spotlight was no longer on me. I was glad of that.

That afternoon our final exhibition game with the Dodgers got under way before a crowd of fourteen thousand fans. It was a nip and tuck battle up to the fourth inning, when we scored four runs to take the lead. The Dodgers came right back and scored two to make it 4 to 2. In the fifth inning we were threatening to score again. We had a man on first and nobody out. I came up, determined to drive the runner home. Ervin Palica was pitching for Brooklyn. I hadn't had a hit in my two previous trips to the plate. I just *had* to come through with one this time! So — I promptly hit into an easy — very

121

easy — double play. That killed our rally, and the fans who were pulling for us groaned.

By all the laws of human nature and baseball, I should have been utterly disgusted. I should have kicked at the dirt, hurled my cap down, and shaken my head all the way back to the dugout. Instead, I was smiling from ear to ear. And so was almost everyone in the Montreal dugout. People sitting in the stands must have thought we were crazy. They had just seen me hit into a double play, and here were my teammates congratulating me, shaking my hand, and I was still grinning all over the place. The fans sitting behind our dugout looked on in utter amazement.

Well, it had at last come to pass. Mr. Rickey had done exactly what he said he was going to do on April 10. At the very moment I had hit into that double play, Arthur Mann, assistant to Mr. Rickey, was passing out an announcement in the press box. It was tersely worded: "The Brooklyn Dodgers today purchased the contract of Jackie Roosevelt Robinson from the Montreal Royals."

Bedlam reigned in the press box. Reporters were making mad dashes for the telephones. Stories were being flashed across the nation and even around the world.

I was — at long last — a big leaguer! I was a member of the Brooklyn Dodgers!

I'm a Bum

WHEN I WAS TOSSED OUT AT FIRST BASE IN THAT DOUBLE play, I automatically turned toward the Montreal dugout. I could see the players on the bench. One of them was going through a series of hysterical gestures, first pointing to me and then to the Brooklyn dugout. That's when I broke into a grin. I knew then that the announcement of my signing had been made and that the news had drifted down from the press box to the bench. My Montreal teammates' obvious delight over my good fortune made me all the happier.

I knew, of course, that the announcement would be made sometime during the game. That morning, while I was still sound asleep in my room at the McAlpin, the phone rang. I grabbed for the receiver like a drowning man clutching for a rope.

"Hello," I managed through the fog of sleep lodged in my throat.

"Good morning," a feminine voice answered. "This is Mr. Rickey's secretary. He wants you to get over here right away and sign your contract. You're now on the Dodgers."

Some writers have called me the fastest man in baseball. That, of course, is a matter of conjecture. But on that morning of April 10, there was no doubt about it. I set some kind of world record for getting dressed. In less time than it takes to tell, I was on my way to the office of the Brooklyn Dodgers. One hour later, surrounded by Mr. Rickey and his immediate staff, I signed my contract and became the first Negro in modern times to enter the "sacred portals" of the Major Leagues.

That's just how it happened — with neatness and dispatch and no fanfare whatever. Simple, wasn't it? It could have happened to you. The telephone rings. You answer it . . . and you're in the Big Leagues. . . . Just like a fairy tale. . . . Cinderella woke up one morning married to a handsome prince. . . . I went to bed one night wearing pajamas and woke up wearing a Brooklyn Dodgers' uniform.

Of course, it hadn't been that easy. But when it happens, it seems that way. You say to yourself: "It wasn't necessary to do all that worrying, now was it?"

As soon as the exhibition game with Brooklyn was over, I rushed for the dressing room. When I walked in, the fellows all slapped me on the back and continued to congratulate me. Clay Hopper shook my hand and said, "I knew we couldn't keep you long. I sure wanted to, but this is your big chance. Now go out there and make good. I know you can." That was Clay Hopper, the manager from Mississippi, talking — the man I had once feared might be one of the obstacles in my attempt to make the Majors. In his slow, pronounced Southern drawl, he was wishing me luck, making it clear he liked me, assuring me I was Major League caliber.

Then the newspapermen flooded the room. They asked me how it felt to be in the Big Leagues.

"It feels wonderful, even if I haven't ever played in the Big Leagues yet," I said. "I just hope I can justify everybody's faith in me."

"This means a lot in many ways," one reporter informed me.

"Believe me," I said, "I fully realize what it means — my being given this opportunity — not only for me, but for my race and for baseball. I'm grateful to Mr. Rickey for the chance, and I'll do my level best to come through in every way."

I was elated over my advancement to the Dodgers. But, strangely, not as much as when I had been signed by Montreal. The Montreal opportunity had come as a complete surprise — out of nowhere; whereas elevation to the Dodgers became a possibility the day I joined Montreal. For more than a year now, I had been dreaming and hoping and even believing I'd eventually make the Dodgers. But the Montreal offer had been a stunning piece of good fortune — one I could never quite believe in even after it was a fact.

Meanwhile, in the midst of all this excitement, Clyde Sukeforth had been named temporary manager of the Dodgers. I was mighty happy over that. I knew that he was definitely in my corner. After all, he was the scout Rickey had sent to get me in 1945 when I was playing in Chicago with the Kansas City Monarchs. And all through my efforts to make good he had been my friend and advisor. I think he wanted me to succeed almost as much as my wife and mother did. Clyde Sukeforth is a wonderful man. Many times during spring training I used to say: "I wish Sukey was the Brooklyn manager. I'd bet he'd ask Mr. Rickey to bring me up." Durocher was the manager then. I liked him, too, but I didn't know him very well, and didn't know what he thought of me. Later, I found out that he had asked Mr. Rickey to make a first baseman out of me. He wanted me on the Dodgers. But I didn't know that then. I just wished Sukeforth had the job. I was sure that if I was ever promoted, he'd be for me all the way.

So when I walked out on the field the next day to play first base against the New York Yankees in an exhibition game at Ebbets Field, I was working under the man who first took me to Brooklyn. "Now don't get nervous,"

125

Sukey said. "Just go out there and play ball like you know how. There's no need to be nervous."

"Oh, I'm not nervous," I lied. I could hardly keep my voice from trembling!

When I started out for the park that morning, I was concerned about the reception I would be given in the dressing room. Would I be welcome, or would my new teammates be cool and aloof — or even ignore me? Before I opened the dressing room door I stopped, took a deep breath, and then walked in. Many of the players were there already. I looked for a locker with "Jackie Robinson" on it, but couldn't find one. I stood in the middle of the room for a while wondering what to do. There were lockers there marked: "Pee Wee Reese," "Dixie Walker," "Hugh Casey," "Ed Stanky," "Bruce Edwards," "Pete Reiser," "Ralph Branca," "Arky Vaughan," and "John Jorgenson." In fact, there were lockers for everyone but me.

Finally, the club house man saw me. "Jackie," he said, "you'll have to wait a few days until we can get a locker for you." He handed me my uniform. "Dress over there, if you don't mind." He pointed to a folding chair. I sat down on my "locker" and started dressing.

Meantime, the rest of the players were coming in. A few nodded and said hello; others paid no attention to me. Clyde Sukeforth came in then and took me around to introduce me to each man. Some shook my hand and wished me good luck; others just said hello. The reception was neither cool nor warm. I guess you'd call it on the formal side.

I finally got dressed and looked at myself in the mirror. I was wearing a brand new uniform — No. 42. It fit me and was comfortable, but I still felt like a stranger, or an uninvited guest. I hoped I wouldn't have to face the photographer when I left the dressing room, but they were just outside, ready to fire away with their flash bulbs. As I walked onto the field, the fans recognized me and began to cheer. I loved them all. Here were people who were glad to see me — people with a warm welcome for me.

Soon the game got under way, and there I was playing with and against many of the great ball players of the day. I didn't get any hits, but I at least made no errors; and we beat the Yanks 14 to 6.

The next day the Yanks pitched Allie Reynolds and he was tough. I got one of the two hits he gave up, but they beat us 8 to 1.

Ed Stanky was the first Dodger to try to help me get the hang of my new job. From his second-base position, he began telling me how to play each man. "Move a little to your right, Jackie. This guy hits to left, so swing around," he would shout. I soon found out that Stanky is one of the smartest ball players in the game. He studies each player closely and knows just what he is likely to do.

We opened the 1947 season on April 15 against the Braves. A roaring crowd of 25,000 saw us win the game 5 to 3. I went hitless, but two days later I had the satisfaction of poling my first home run in the Majors. We were playing the Giants at the Polo Grounds, and in the third inning I hit one off the scoreboard in left field. My satisfaction was short-lived, however. The Giants beat us that day 10 to 4.

In those early days of the season, there was considerable speculation as to whether or not I'd be able to make the grade. My hitting was spotty and I certainly was no Fancy Dan at first base. We had two first basemen sitting on the bench — Ed Stevens and Howie Schultz. They had divided the job the season before and both of them were ready to take over if I flopped. I knew that, of course, and I was trying hard to win the job.

Even though I was off to a slow start, I was beginning to feel that the other players on the club were not going to be antagonistic toward me. On April 26, the Associated Press accurately reported: "His Big League teammates have accepted him quite as readily as the Minor Leaguers did at Montreal last year. The welcome has not been an effusive one, for ball players are a group of individualists who think first of their own base hits. But there has been no unpleasantness about Robinson's advent, and several players who were willing to discuss Jackie said there would be none." That aspect, at least, was encouraging.

By this time, Burt Shotton had been named manager. I liked him right away. Mr. Shotton is a quiet, conservative man. He knows his baseball and how to handle his men. When we met for the first time, he shook hands and said: "I've heard a lot about you, Jackie. Keep up the good work." That's about all he said, too.

The first racial "incident" occurred in April, when the Phillies came to Brooklyn for a three-game series. The Phillies, led by their very able manager, Ben Chapman, are great bench-riders. The first time I stepped up to the plate, they opened up full blast. "Hey, you black Nigger," I heard one of them yell. "Why don't you go back where you came from?" Then I heard another one shout: "Yeah, pretty soon you'll want to eat and sleep with white ball players!" As the jockeying continued on this level, I almost lost my head. I started to drop my bat and go over and take a sock at one of them. But then I remembered Branch Rickey's warning me of what I'd have to take without losing my temper. So I pretended I didn't hear them. I gritted my teeth and vented some of my anger on a solid single.

The Phillies' performance eventually reached the ears of the newspapermen, and they lost no time in raking Chapman and his players over the coals. Chapman replied that his club wasn't riding me any harder than the rest of the Dodgers. "Do you want us to go easy on him?" Chapman asked. "They rode me when I came to the

I nearly had a set-to with Joe Garagiola, the St. Louis catcher. He made a crack about my race and we had some hot words, but the umpire stepped between us. I backed up and let Joe argue with the umpire.

Brooklyn turned out in grand style to welcome us after we had clinched the 1947 National League pennant. Here we are in front of Borough Hall as I was given the Rookie of the Year award (circle).

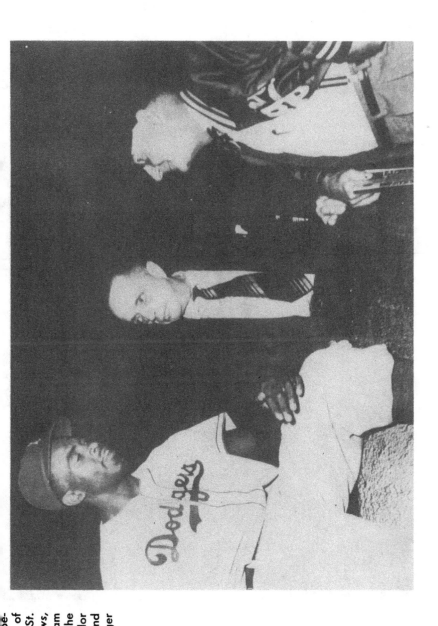

ceived in 1947 was being named Rookie of the Year by the *St. Louis Sporting News*, baseball's bible. I am chatting here with the editor, J. G. Taylor Spink, of the *News*, and Burt Shotten, manager of the Dodgers.

131

The Baseball Writers' Association, Chicago Chapter, presented me with this beautiful memorial award in recognition of my selection as the Rookie of the Year. Jack Ryan made the presentation on November 12, 1947.

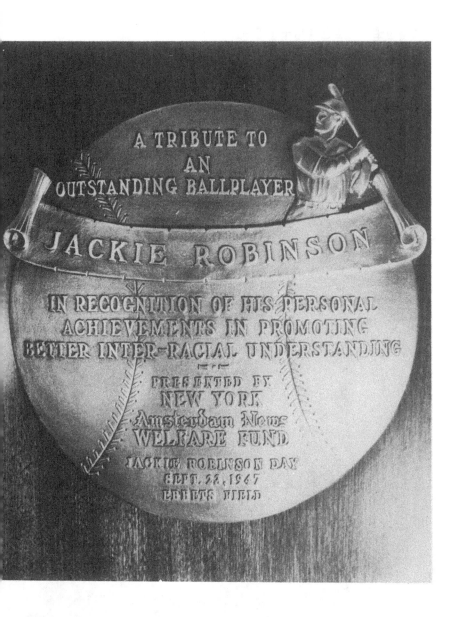

A TRIBUTE TO
AN
OUTSTANDING BALLPLAYER

JACKIE ROBINSON

IN RECOGNITION OF HIS PERSONAL
ACHIEVEMENTS IN PROMOTING
BETTER INTER-RACIAL UNDERSTANDING

PRESENTED BY
NEW YORK
Amsterdam News
WELFARE FUND
JACKIE ROBINSON DAY
SEPT. 23, 1947
EBBETS FIELD

Here is the plaque which the *Amsterdam News* presented to me on "Jackie Robinson Day." I will always treasure it.

The fans at Ebbets Field were swell to me all season long. On September 23, 1947, after we had clinched the pennant, they held a "Jackie Robinson Day," and presented me with a television set, a $500 watch, and many other gifts. The biggest of all was this beautiful Cadillac sedan. Bill "Bojangles" Robinson—no relative—made the presentation.

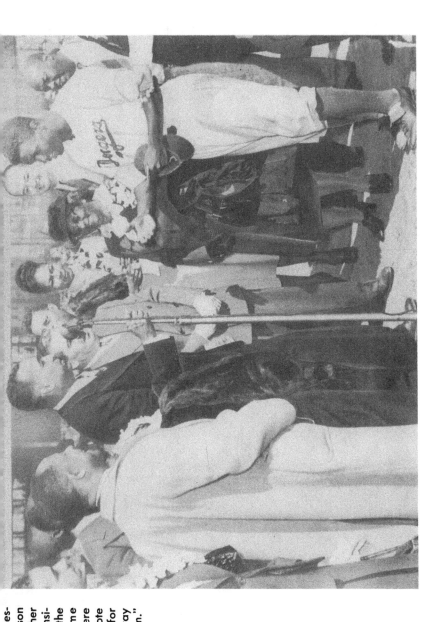

and wife could be present on "Jackie Robinson Day." I told Ma her prayers were responsible for our winning the pennant. One time when the Dodgers were in a slight slump, I wrote her: "Quit praying for me alone, Ma, and pray for the whole team." She did.

135

Playing in the World Series in my first year in the Majors was a great thrill. In the first inning of the first game, I tried to go from second to third on a grounder by Pete Reiser, but was caught on the base path. I kept running back and forth between Yankee pitcher Frank Shea and shortstop Phil Rizzuto. Rizzuto finally tagged me out but I had delayed the play long enough

I was involved in many close plays at first base. In the third inning of the fourth World Series game, I just beat Larry "Yogi" Berra, Yankee catcher, to the bag after I had stopped his grounder.

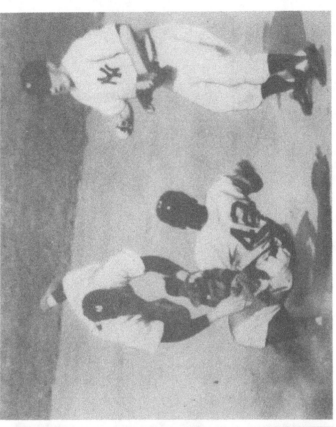

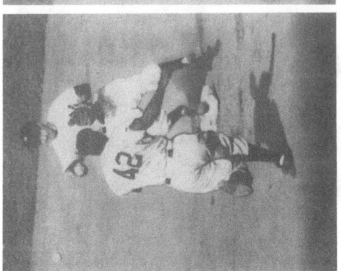

In the sixth game of the World Series, we had the bases loaded when Dixie Walker grounded to Phil Rizzuto. I dashed down to second and did my best to break up a double play. I hit the bag hard and Rizzuto tumbled over my shoulder.

I tried several times to cross up the Yankees in the Series by laying down bunts when they expected me to hit away. But, this time, the ball rolled foul.

It seemed to me that whenever I looked up out of the dugout during the Series, kids were hanging over the roof asking for autographs.

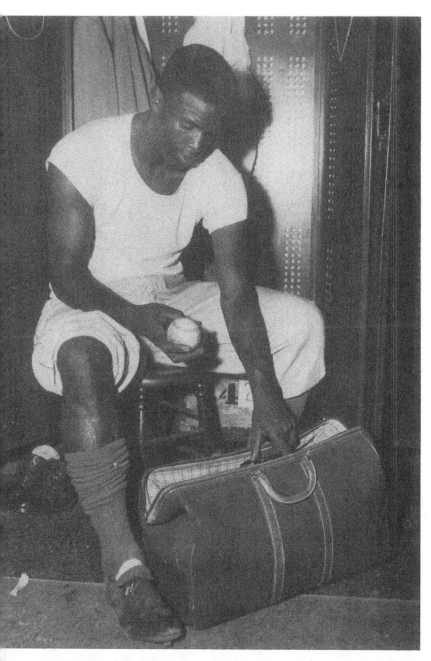

After the World Series, I was looking forward eagerly to a long winter vacation and then another season with the Dodgers. It is the best job I have ever had and I am going to try to keep it for a long time.

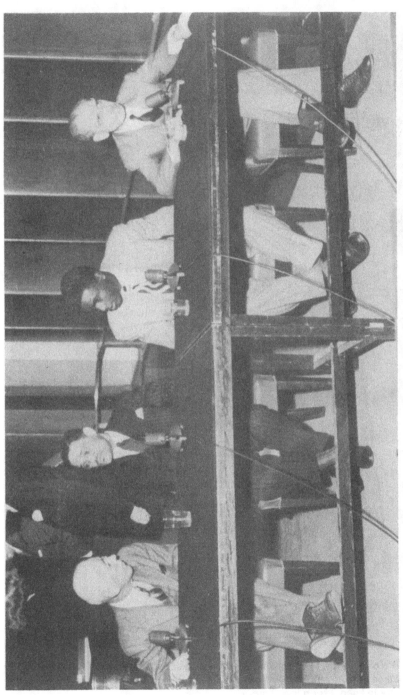

I was pretty lucky when I broke into radio. It happened that I knew quite a few answers on the "Information Please" program, where I was invited to appear with (left to right) John Kieran, Dr. Rufus Clement and Franklin P. Adams.

After the 1947 season, I made some stage appearances. This one was in the Apollo Theatre in New York City, with Monty Hawley.

143

After the 1947 season I almost became a movie star. One of the Hollywood producers had me on the movie lot and took a few shots. But there was not time enough to make a complete movie before training began for the 1948 season and I was obliged to leave for the Dominican Republic.

Majors, and we're not going to be any different than players in the past when it comes to bench-jockeying." Chapman told Jack Saunders, *Pittsburgh Courier* representative in Philadelphia, that he had instructed his players to call me everything and anything they wanted to.

Later on, it was reported that Commissioner Chandler had warned the Phillies that they'd have to leave out the racial epithets when they were riding me.

I imagine one of the reasons the issue became a matter of official concern was because Walter Winchell blasted the Phillies on his Sunday night radio program and in his widely read column. Once again the press had come to my defense.

The next time we played the Phillies they kept their verbal blows above the belt. I posed for a picture with Manager Ben Chapman and the whole thing died, thank goodness. "Jackie has been accepted in baseball and we of the Philadelphia organization have no objection to his playing and wish him all the luck we can," Chapman told newspapermen after that series.

It was along about this time, also, that the St. Louis strike story broke. The Cardinals, it was reported, weren't going to play against me when they came to Brooklyn. (I tell this story in detail in the next chapter.) And in addition I was receiving some pretty ugly letters through the mails. Mr. Rickey turned two of them over to the New York police and they investigated. Naturally, the senders used assumed names and false addresses.

I don't think I can be accused of offering an alibi now if I say that these things affected my ball playing. I was doing all right in the field, but my batting average was still slipping. In fact, it was going down like an elevator in the Empire State Building. Eddie Stevens was now playing with Montreal, but Howie Schultz was still with us. I was sure that any day Bert Shotton would say:

145

"Jackie, you'd better sit it out awhile. I think I'll use Howie today."

But on May 10, the Brooklyn Club gave me a vote of confidence. They sold Howie Schultz to the Phillies for 50,000 dollars. We were in a three-game losing streak then, and I wasn't doing much to help get us back in the win column. Boston and Chicago were tied for first place; we were in third place, one game behind. That same night in Philadelphia I started clicking. We lost an eleven-inning heart-breaker to the Phillies 6 to 5, but I got some satisfaction out of doubling, singling, and scoring two runs. . . . "You should be ready to go at top speed now," Clyde Sukeforth told me after the game. "You looked loose up there tonight, not tight like you have been."

The first real words of encouragement I received from a player on an opposing team came seven days later from Hank Greenberg of the Pittsburgh Pirates. We were playing the Pirates at Ebbets Field and Hank was at first base. I hit a ball to shortstop and the throw to first was wide. Just as I rounded the sack, Greenberg threw his big arm across my path in a desperate effort to catch the ball. Naturally, we collided and I was knocked down. The ball rolled into short right field and I had time to get up and continue on to second.

The next inning Hank came to bat and got a walk. When he got to first base, he said, "Did I hurt you on that play last inning, Jackie?"

"No, Hank," I answered, "I'm okay."

"I was stretching to get the ball," he said. "I didn't mean to knock you down."

"That's all right," I assured him. "I tried to get out of your way too, but I couldn't."

The big handsome Pirate slugger smiled and said, "Listen, don't pay any attention to these guys who are trying to make it hard for you. Stick in there. You're doing fine. The next time you come to Pittsburgh, I hope you and I can get together for a talk. There are a few things I've learned down through the years that might help you and make it easier."

I thanked him from the bottom of my heart. Those words of encouragement helped me tremendously. I knew that he was sincere because I had heard he had experienced some racial trouble when he came up. I felt sure that he understood my problems. I liked him, too. The man had class, Hank Greenberg did.

By June 27 we were in first place by half a game. Boston and the Giants were hot on our heels. We were playing good ball and had won eight out of nine games on the road. I was beginning to adjust myself to Major League baseball, too, and it made me happy to find that most sportswriters now felt that I had measured up to Big League standards. For instance, here's an International News Service story I read in a Boston paper one morning:

"The time has come to recognize Jackie Robinson, Brooklyn's first baseman, as a Major League ball player who has come through under extreme pressure to become an important factor in the Dodgers' rise to the National League lead.

"Batting .302 after last night's 8-6 thrilling victory over Boston, Robinson deserves to be rated with the best rookies of the season, although he never played first base before the Brooks hit Panama during Spring training.

"Through the West, it was Robinson's batting that started the club on a victory string which now measures 8 out of 9. In Pittsburgh he stole home against Fritz Ostermueller with a tie-breaking run. After Boston, fighting desperately for first place, rallied for five runs to tie the Dodgers 6-6 last night, Robinson's eighth-inning double started the victorious two-run splurge.

"Over a stretch of the last nine games, Robinson has

batted .326 and has been scoring so often he now is second in the league with 52, topped only by Johnny Mize. He leads the league in stolen bases with 10. He has hit safely in 12 straight games."

I was particularly pleased over doing well in Boston because, as you recall, it was in this city that I had first "tried out" for a Major League club. That had been two years previously, and the Red Sox had brushed me off without any semblance of a fair trial. I was still piqued over that snub. I knew it was childish, but I found myself wishing the Red Sox were in the National League and the Braves in the American. "Then," I told myself, "I could really show Joe Cronin what a mistake he'd made!"

Meantime, things began to break better for me all the way around. My own teammates were becoming accustomed to me and even the players on the other teams were much more pleasant. Reese, Reiser, Barney, Branca, Casey, Bragan, Edwards, Hermanski, and Jorgenson were especially nice to me. Anyway my fan mail was no longer abusive. For instance, a Chicagoan wrote:

> May I salute you and wish you luck on your
> newest venture?
> I hope you bust the league wide open with
> base hits this year. Good luck. You're a credit
> to all races; or, better, to the human race.
> > Gordon Brooks
> P.S.—A 'Bum' fan and a white man.

A letter from a Southern fan read:

> Jackie: I am a white man, who like many
> thousands of other white people, feel that
> in our American way of life we should not
> tolerate race prejudice and that a person
> will be judged on his merits. I send you
> congratulations and believe you will be

148

a credit to baseball, just as Joe Louis has
been to boxing.

The most unique letter I received came from Portland,
Oregon:

> Hi, Black Boy: Glad to know that you have
> arrived. Had good idea that you had the
> stuff and would make good in the Big
> Leagues. You are a credit to your race—the
> human race, son. Very glad to see you in the
> Majors. Good luck!
>
> Sincerely,
> WHITE BOY

The last of June, we were swinging through the West,
heading for a pennant. Much of the original pressure
was off me and I was playing better ball. When I first
joined the club, I constantly felt that people looked
on me as a curiosity. But by now both players and fans
were getting used to me. I didn't feel like a sideshow
freak any more. Better still, I was beginning to feel that
I was really an important part of the team. No one on the
club seemed to resent my presence any more. All of us
were getting the pennant fever, and the team became
closer and more unified than it had ever been.

On the trains I now became a part of the bull ses-
sions. I played cards now and then and sometimes joined
in kidding one of the boys who had pulled a boner during
a game. They kidded me, too. One day in Chicago a Cub
batter socked a sizzling grounder down the first base
line. It came so fast I didn't have time to bend over for
it. The ball hit my feet and stopped dead but I thought
it had gone through me. I looked around wildly for it,
but couldn't see it. Then I suddenly looked up in the
air. Maybe it had shot upwards when it hit my feet. I
scanned the skies above for the lost ball.

149

Meantime, the base runner was well on his way to second. Reese was standing on second, waiting to take the throw. Eddie Stanky was screaming at me: "Look *down*, Jack," he pleaded, "look *down*! The ball's right at your feet!"

But the crowd was screaming, too, and I was utterly confused. I could not make out what Stanky was saying, and I couldn't find that ball.

Finally I discovered it, but by that time the base runner was perched on second, laughing at me as though he had just seen an Al Schacht pantomime. . . . I guess he had, at that!

After the game we headed for Brooklyn. I was sitting in my room on the train, thinking about the dumb play I had made, when Hugh Casey, a wonderful fellow and a great pitcher, wandered in.

"Jackie," he said with a serious expression on his heavy-set face, "we're getting you that new glove when we get to Brooklyn."

"What new glove?" I asked, puzzled, "I haven't ordered a new glove."

"Well," Casey said, "we've decided to get you another glove."

"What am I going to do with a new glove, Hugh?"

"Why we're gonna put it on your foot," Casey revealed with a roar of laughter. "You won't even have to bend over for a ball then."

Both of us had a good laugh, especially when Casey demonstrated how I looked when that ball was between my feet.

After Casey left, I kept laughing to myself. But not over my bonehead play. I was laughing with joy because I knew now that I was one of Brooklyn's beloved Bums. . . .

I could hear the fans in Brooklyn shouting at me: "Come on, hit the ball, ya Bum!"

S *trike!*

IT WAS AS INEVITABLE AS NIGHT FOLLOWS DAY THAT MY presence in the Major Leagues would eventually be challenged, officially or unofficially, by some group within or without the ranks of baseball. From the time I joined Montreal until the day it actually happened, that certainty loomed before me like a pirate about to swoop down upon his prize.

Instead of a pirate, however, it was a Cardinal!

The challenge was short-lived, thanks to the League officials and the press; after it was over, I was more firmly entrenched than ever.

It happened in the early part of May, 1947. We were in a battle for first place with four other clubs. The St. Louis Cardinals were coming to town and we were grooming for the crucial struggle with our ancient and aggressive rivals. Before the St. Louis club reached Brooklyn, however, it was rumored that the Cardinals were going to stage a strike against me. The papers reported that the St. Louis players had agreed among themselves that they would not play Brooklyn with me in the line-up.

As early as October of 1945, there were indications that trouble might be brewing. In that month the United Press released a story which contained the alleged views of certain baseball players and officials who were reported to be opposed to the "Rickey experiment." First of those quoted was one of the most popular players on the Brook-

151

lyn club. Said the United Press: "Fred 'Dixie' Walker, star Brooklyn outfielder who was born in Georgia and now lives in Birmingham, Alabama, said: 'As long as he isn't with the Dodgers, I'm not worried.' "

I prefer to believe that Dixie never said that. Approximately two years after the alleged statement was made, I was with the Dodgers. I never saw any evidence that Dixie was "worried." He was always courteous and considerate to me. Never once, by word or deed, did he indicate that he resented my presence on the Brooklyn club.

Continuing, the United Press story said: "There was the same implication of sharp disapproval by other Southern players if the situation arose where Robinson or any other Negro actually would reach the Major Leagues. Coach Spud Davis of the Pirates and Elmer Riddle of Cincinnati, both from the South, also remarked: 'It's all right as long as they're with some other team.' "

George Digby, Boston Red Sox scout, was far more outspoken when interviewed in New Orleans. "Personally," he told the United Press, "I think it's the worst thing that can happen to organized baseball. I think a lot of Southern boys will refuse to compete with Negroes in baseball, just as they have in other sports. The Negroes have had their own league all these years and have operated successfully. I don't think anyone should go in and start a lot of trouble — especially at this time."

Rogers Hornsby, who rose to baseball greatness from the sandlots of Texas, was just as definite in his opposition to Negro players in the white Minor or Major Leagues.

"The Negro Leagues," he was quoted as saying, "are doing all right and Negro players should be developed and then remain as stars in their own leagues. A mixed ball team differs from other sports because ball players on the road live much closer. I think Branch Rickey was wrong in signing Robinson to play with Montreal and it won't work out."

The above are but a few of the alleged statements. I cannot verify any of them, nor did I ever have any wish to try. I was happy to read, after the story appeared, that some of the people named emphatically stated that they had been misquoted. Nevertheless I knew that such a story, whether based largely on rumor or not, was sure to mean some rough sledding ahead. Much to my surprise, nothing untoward happened while I was in the International League — nothing, that is, in the form of an organized boycott by players or others who resented my presence.

Then, approximately a month after I had been in the Majors, the air grew tense with rumors of a strike against me. I heard them, of course, but didn't say anything; I just kept on playing the best ball I could, telling myself that if it happened, a lot of people would be on my side.

On May 9, the story exploded in the press. The New York *Herald Tribune,* in a copyrighted article by Sports Editor Stanley Woodward, told the sports world the story of the threatened strike. "A National League players strike," Mr. Woodward wrote, "instigated by some of the St. Louis Cardinals, against the presence in the league of Jackie Robinson, Negro first baseman, has been averted temporarily and perhaps squashed.

"In recent days Ford Frick, President of the National League, and Sam Breadon, President of the St. Louis club, have been conferring with St. Louis players in the Hotel New Yorker. Mr. Breadon flew East when he heard of the projected strike. The story that he came to consult with Eddie Dyer, manager, about the lowly state of the St. Louis club was fictitious. He came on a much more serious errand."

Mr. Woodward said the strike, though organized by certain St. Louis players, had been instigated by a member of the Brooklyn Dodgers who had later recanted. The original plan called for a St. Louis club strike on May 6, the day of their first game of the year in Brooklyn.

"Subsequently, the St. Louis players," he wrote, "conceived the idea of a general strike within the National League on a certain date. That is what Frick and Breadon have been combating the last few days."

Then Woodward quoted a statement that Ford Frick allegedly sent the St. Louis players. It has been called one of the most emphatic, clear-cut, and *uncompromising* mandates ever issued in the history of baseball.

"If you do this," Mr. Frick warned, "you will be suspended from the League. You will find that the friends you think you have in the press box will not support you, that you will be outcasts. I do not care if half the League strikes. Those who do it will encounter quick retribution.

"All will be suspended and I don't care if it wrecks the National League.

"This is the United States of America, and one citizen has as much right to play as another.

"The National League will go down the line with Robinson, whatever the consequences. You will find if you go through with your intention that you have been guilty of complete madness."

Mr. Woodward insisted that the story had been thoroughly substantiated. "The St. Louis players involved," he wrote, "unquestionably will deny it. We doubt, however, that Frick or Breadon will go that far. A return of 'No comment' from either or both will serve as confirmation.

"It is generally known," he continued, "that other less serious difficulties have attended elevation of Robinson to the Major Leagues. Through it all, Robinson, whose intelligence and degree of education are far beyond that of the average ball player, has behaved himself in an exemplary manner."

The following day, according to the Associated Press, President Ford Frick declined to comment further on the alleged strike. He said the subject was a dead issue and that "a mountain had been made out of a molehill anyway."

Breadon and his manager, Eddie Dyer, both denied that the Cardinals had threatened a strike. Breadon did admit, however, that there was some dissatisfaction among National League players — not the Cardinals — over my presence in the Majors.

"I decided to talk the thing over with some of the men," Mr. Breadon said, "because it would be such a terrible thing. I brought the matter up with two of my leading players. They never intimated that such a thing was even thought of."

The Associated Press then said: "It was learned that the 'two leading players' were Terry Moore and Marty Marion, the club's representatives on the baseball players' committee, and that both denied knowledge of any strike plan."

Manager Dyer said that at no time, to his knowledge, did his players consider such foolish action. He added that if Brooklyn wanted to use me against the Cardinals, it was certainly all right with him and his players.

Many of the leading sportswriters rallied to my support during this critical period. Tom Meany of the newspaper *PM,* for instance, said that if any player in the National League was so bigoted that the idea of playing against me was repellent to him, he should look for another job and profession.

Doubtless there were some players on other clubs in the League who also were opposed to Negroes playing in the Majors. I learned on good authority, for instance, that while the Chicago Cubs were training at Catalina Island, a member of the team told a sportswriter that he was going to urge his teammates to strike against me. That, by the way, occurred before I was brought up to Brooklyn. Well, there was no strike, and when the newspaperman asked the instigator what happened to his plan, he said: "The boys just wouldn't co-operate, and I don't want to be a loner."

I think it should be pointed out that a refusal to play against me would have been sheer hypocrisy. In the off-season, Major Leaguers have barnstormed all over the continent, playing with and against Negro players.

And so the talk of strike threats died away. We played our early May series with the Cards without any overt bad feeling. By and large, the Cardinals treated me as merely another ball player. They were a rough, tough, fighting ball club, never licked till the last man was out. They tried to beat us with every legitimate tactic known to baseball, but toward the end of the season some writers thought several of the Cards were out to "get me."

In its report on the incipient strike, the Associated Press named Marty Marion as one of the leaders. Maybe he was, but it's hard for me to believe. Here's why. About the middle of the season we were in St. Louis for an important series. In the first game, I got a single, and a moment later stole second. Joe Garagiola, the Card's catcher, threw high and Marion had to jump to get the ball. When he came down he landed on my legs, which were sprawled across the bag.

As I stood up, Marion said, "Did I hurt you, Jackie?"

"No," I said, "I'm all right, Marty."

"That's good," he said with a smile. "I've got new spikes on my shoes. If they'd got you, it would have been a bad cut. I'm glad you're okay."

The next hitter singled over second and I went all the way home with the winning run. While I was racing for the plate I can remember saying to myself: "Nice guy, that Marty Marion, nice guy."

Winning the Pennant

IN AUGUST WE HAD ANOTHER CRUCIAL SWING THROUGH THE West. If we could play .500 ball, we had an excellent chance to win the pennant. We had to play a series with each of the four Western clubs — Pittsburgh, Chicago, Cincinnati, and St. Louis. The tension was high, especially in St. Louis and Chicago, and as a result I encountered some pretty rough going.

On a Saturday night in Sportsman's Park, St. Louis, a capacity crowd was on hand to see us battle the Cards. In the sixth inning we were behind, 7 to 0. Harry (The Cat) Brecheen was on the mound. He was having it easy, throwing up slow twisters and dinky curves that we could not hit for love nor money. When I came to bat, I swung at one of those dinkies and topped the ball between the pitcher's mound and first base. Brecheen leaped on the ball, picked it up, and then stood squarely astride the base line, waiting to tag me.

But I didn't know he was there. I was running head down and hard as I could go for first base. When I did look up and see him squarely in my path, I was burned up. He had plenty of time to throw the ball to first base for an easy out. Brecheen knew as well as I did that any other player would have run over him and knocked him down in the hope that he'd drop the ball. But, of course, that was the sort of thing I'd been told to avoid. I stopped dead on the base line. He tagged me.

157

I couldn't help saying something to him, however. "You better play your position like you're supposed to," I said. "Next time, I'm going to dump you on the back of your lap!"

Brecheen said something back to me, but I was so angry I didn't hear him.

That was the first time I had ever actually lost my temper on the field. It was also the first time I had ever said an angry word to an opposing player. When I got back to the bench, Jack Pitler, one of our coaches, said, "He should have been dumped on his rump, but I guess you can't afford to do that, Jackie."

That was only one of the unpleasant incidents in that series. On a close play at first base, Enos Slaughter slid into me and practically tore my shoe off. I don't think he did it intentionally, but some of the sportswriters assumed that he had. He said later that I had taken too much of the bag. I didn't think so, but in all fairness to him I should report that there had been some talk around the league that I was taking too much room on first base when I tagged the bag. In fact, Andy Pafko had told a Chicago newspaperman: "I realize Robinson is new at the position and learning it as he goes along. But he'll have to watch his tagging foot. I nearly nicked him once because he took much of the bag. The runner has the right-of-way going over first, and Robinson can avoid a possible spiking if he keeps his foot on the side of the sack."

Finally, I nearly had a set-to with Joe Garagiola, the St. Louis catcher. On one of my trips to the plate, he made a crack about my race. We had some hot words, and for a moment it looked as though we would come to blows; but the umpire stepped between us, and at the same moment my "personal body guard," Clyde Sukeforth, came dashing out of the dugout to "save" me. The ump nearly banished him from the bench for his pains, but the game proceeded peacefully.

When we moved into Chicago, we were all set to mop up the Cubs if we possibly could. On our last Chicago visit, they had licked us in three important games. And sure enough, we did flatten them in three straight games. On the fourth day, the Cubs were in a ugly mood. In the ninth inning of that final game, I led off with a single. Bill Lee was pitching for the Cubs, and I tried to worry him. He tried to hold me close to first, but on the third pitch I stole second. Then I took a big lead off second to try to get Lee upset again. Len Merullo, the Cub shortstop, kept sneaking in behind me, trying to catch me off the bag.

Suddenly Lee whirled and whipped a throw to Merullo who was already on the bag. I made a desperate slide for the bag, sailing right between Merullo's legs. When he caught the ball, he fell on top of me. The umpire called me safe, and that made the Cub shortstop furious. As he got up, he booted me with his knee.

That made me mad, of course, and I started to swing at him. But once again, I somehow had presence of mind enough to hold my temper. If I tangled with Merullo, I knew it would probably end up in a general free-for-all. The crowd of twenty thousand was yelling and the players of both clubs were up off the benches, standing on the dugout steps. So I got up and started dusting off my uniform. "Mr. Rickey would have convulsions," I told myself, "if you started a fight with this guy." Merullo was still standing by, glaring at me. He was ready for anything. The umpire was still standing by, too, afraid there was going to be trouble. Finally, Lee returned to his pitching chores and the game went on. I was still so mad that I had a crazy impulse to steal third and then home. But I knew I'd never make it — they were watching me too closely.

About six weeks later, the Cubs came to Brooklyn. Before the game both teams were riding each other from the bench. Merullo was one of the leaders. He was baiting practically everyone of our bench. Finally Eddie Stanky, who has a cutting tongue, yelled over to him: "Listen, Merullo, why don't you jump on somebody who can fight you back?"

Merullo knew that Stanky was talking about the way he had roughed me up in Chicago. I guess he wasn't prepared for that crack, because it shut him up for the moment.

And then there was one brief explosion in Cincinnati. The Reds' great pitcher, Ewell Blackwell, had reached the ninth inning without giving up a base hit. He got the first two men out and Eddie Stanky came up. Blackwell was just one away from every pitcher's dream — a no-hit game. But the pesky Stanky singled and ruined his no-hitter. When I stepped up, Blackwell was hotter than the Fourth of July in the tropics. In his exasperation and disappointment, he launched a blast of profanity and name-calling at me.

"Come on," I demanded, "pitch the ball."

He wound up and threw a fast ball that I drove sharply to right field for a base hit. I suppose that merely rubbed salt in the wound, but so it goes in a ball game. . . .

Naturally, such incidents as I have related hurt and anger me, but I think I understand why they occur. In the excitement and heat of a hard-fought game, every nerve in a player's body is keyed to the breaking point. Then something snaps inside, and a good-natured guy suddenly goes berserk for a few seconds. Old, long-buried prejudices and racial epithets subconsciously leap to the surface. I believe most of us are sorry and ashamed after such outbursts, and I'm certain they will happen less and less frequently in America — both in the ball park and outside.

When we started on that last Western swing, we were five and a half games in front. When we got back to Brooklyn we had increased our lead to eight games and just about cinched the pennant. In fact, the papers had already conceded it to us, and the Brooklyn office had started selling World Series tickets.

Despite the unpleasant incidents in the West, I had played pretty good ball. In ten days on the road I hit .408, made three home runs, and stole five bases. But more gratifying than that was the growing evidence that old, experienced baseball men now considered me a qualified Major Leaguer.

Manager Charley Grimm of the Chicago Cubs called me "the most improved player in the Majors." He said when he saw me for the first time, at the beginning of the season, that he didn't think I'd make the grade. But now he was sure I was a Big Leaguer.

Grimm was probably recalling my twenty consecutive times at bat without a base hit — in those early season days when I had been the "All-American out."

Harold C. Burr, writing in the St. Louis *Sporting News*, said: "No matter what their team fate, when the honor roll of the 1947 Dodgers is called at the conclusion of the National League race, the name of Jackie Robinson will have a high place on the Flatbush hero scroll. He's the best base-runner to come up in either league since Ty Cobb. Once he gets on first and starts to dance around, he has the pitcher crazy and the whole park in an uproar. He has an awkward gait and the first time Manager Burt Shotton watched him on the paths he didn't think Jackie was traveling very fast.

"'Then I put my stopwatch on him,' confessed Burt, who likes to sit on the bench and clock the team around the bases. 'This boy can run, I said to myself.'"

161

Fred Down of the New York *Sun* wrote as follows:

" 'The most improved ball player of the year,' is the consensus of National League managers when the subject of Jackie Robinson, the Dodgers' rookie first baseman, is discussed in the dugout.

"Robinson was not very good when the Dodgers returned from spring training. The Yankees expressed amazement when they saw him at first base in the three-game series between the Dodgers and Bronxites. They didn't believe the Dodgers could afford to go along with him.

"All that is gone now, however. Jackie knows where — and how — to make all the plays. He is still not expert on some — but his improvement has been rapid, and around the circuit every manager expresses the conviction that he will be one of the League's outstanding first basemen by the end of next year."

I was happy over another development. The fans were treating me magnificently all around the circuit. Kids tore the buttons off my coat when I'd leave the park, and even on foreign fields the fans rooted for me. My own people were the most enthusiastic, of course, but I got plenty of encouragement from white people, too. When we returned from that last Western trip, a mob of people met us at Grand Central Station. They cornered a lot of us and we had to make a run for it. Like a dope, I tried to hide in a telephone booth. They saw me and I was hopelessly trapped. I appreciated the tribute, but I did want to get home to my wife and son. Finally somebody got the police to come and rescue me from that wildly happy throng.

The greatest honor I received during the season was in being named the "Rookie of the Year" by the St. Louis *Sporting News*, baseball's bible, and by the Baseball Writers' Association.

162

Here is what Editor J. G. Taylor Spink of the *News* wrote:

"In selecting the outstanding rookie of 1947, the *Sporting News* sifted and weighed only stark baseball values.

"That Jack Roosevelt Robinson might have had more obstacles than his first-year competitors, and that he perhaps had a harder fight to gain even Major League recognition, was no concern of this publication. The sociological experiment that Robinson represented, the trail-blazing that he did, the barriers he broke down, did not enter into the decision. He was rated and examined solely as a freshman player in the Big Leagues — on the basis of his hitting, his running, his defensive play, his team value.

"Dixie Walker summed it up in a few words the other day when he said: 'No other ball player on this club, with the possible exception of Bruce Edwards, has done more to put the Dodgers up in the race than Robinson has. He is everything Branch Rickey said he was when he came up from Montreal.'

"The record shows that Robinson has laid down 42 successful bunts up to September 9. Fourteen of these were beaten out for hits and 28 were sacrifices. He failed only four times.

"Robinson has been a demon on the bases. So far he has stolen second 19 times, third three times, home three times (on Ostermueller, Pollet, and Beggs), and has been thrown out only nine times. He has stolen against every club in the League.

"Those big shoulders that go into his peculiar sweeping swing have power, too. He has banged nine home runs. He has learned to hit the change of pace on which pitchers were getting him out early in the season. He has been among the leaders all year in the number of hits, and figures to get close to 200 his first season.

"Robinson's play is consistent. On Sunday, September

7, he missed his first game. No other Dodger had played in them all until that date. He has hit .290 on the road and .298 at home for a collective .295. Jackie started slowly, hitting only .225 in April when a lot people quit on him prematurely. He hit .284 in May, got hot in June when he ran up his twenty-one-game hitting streak, getting 43 hits during the month for a .377 average. He was a cool .253 in July, but got going again during August to travel at a clip of .311.

"Jackie Robinson has done it all, in his first year as a Major Leaguer. What more could anyone ask?"

And then to cap it all, a few days before the season ended, a group of Brooklyn and New York fans arranged a "Jackie Robinson Day" at Ebbets Field. They gave me a beautiful Cadillac sedan, a television set, and many other lovely gifts. That was one of the memorable days in my baseball career. There was a big crowd in the stands that day, and when the car was driven out on the field and Bill Robinson, the great dancer, made the presentation, my heart and eyes were running over with gratitude and joy.

When the season ended, I was nineteenth in the official batting average standings. I led the league in stolen bases and in sacrifice hits, was second in runs scored, and tied for fourth place in total number of bases. And I had played in 151 of our 154 games.

Here is my composite record:

G	AB	R	H	TB	2B	3B	HR	RBI	SH	SB	Pct.
151	591	125	175	252	31	5	12	48	28	29	.296

All in all, I had had a very lucky year.

The Best Job I Ever Had

WELL, AS YOU KNOW, WE WON THE PENNANT BY A COM-
fortable margin and went into the World Series
against the Yankees. We lost, but not until the seventh
and final game. It's a great thrill to play in the Series.
Some players are in baseball for fifteen or twenty years
and never get in a World Series. Here I was in it in my
first year. Luck was with me again.

Right in the first inning of the first game, Frank Shea,
the Yankee pitcher, walked me, and I promptly stole
second base. Pete Reiser hit a fast bounder to Phil Rizzuto, Yankee shortstop, and as I had been taking a long
lead, I was trapped between second and third. Shea and
Rizzuto ran me down, but I raced back and forth between them until I saw Reiser safe on second before I
was tagged out. We scored one run that round.

In the third inning, Shea walked me again. He didn't
take any chances on my stealing second. Four times he
tossed to George McQuinn at first to hold me close. I
still kept taking a safe lead, and the fifth time that Shea
started to throw to first, the ball slipped from his hand.
I went down to second on the balk, and the crowd at
the Yankee Stadium was in an uproar.

However, I didn't score, and the Yanks came back in
the fifth to score five runs and sew up the ball game.

Afterwards, some of the sportswriters cornered me and
asked if I had been nervous. They said I showed no signs

165

of the jitters and they were right. "Nothing could be more nerve-wracking," I told them, "than that last series in St. Louis."

Next day was our worst. We had a number of bad breaks in that second game, and I made a couple of awkward plays. I came in fast on a hopper one time, and found that I couldn't beat the batter to first, and no Dodger had been able to cover the bag. I couldn't make any play at all, so I held onto the ball.

I was overanxious on my next chance. It was the seventh inning and the Yanks had the bases loaded, with Allie Reynolds, their pitcher, at bat. We all figured a bunt was coming, and sure enough it came down the first base line right toward me. I was in such a hurry to cut off the run at the plate that I just couldn't pick up the ball. It played croquet between my legs. Billy Johnson scored and Berra reached third on my error. Four Yankee runs scored that inning, and the Yanks won by 10 to 3.

We were all gloomy that night, and the Yanks were beaming with confidence. They had good reason, leading by two games right off the bat. Still, I felt that the Dodgers could win the Series.

After the third game, I was more optimistic and so was everyone else in Brooklyn. Playing at Ebbets Field, with familiar ground under our feet, made a big difference.

I singled to center in the first inning of the third game. When the count on Pete Reiser, next batter, reached three and one, I scooted down to second base. Yank catcher Lollar threw poorly and the ball got past Rizzuto. I rounded second before I noticed that Stirnweiss had backed up the play. I dived for the bag but it was too late, and Rizzuto tagged me out.

In the second, we were luckier. I singled again, sending

Eddie Stanky to third. Then Carl Furillo bounced a long double off the scoreboard, scoring both of us. We wound up with six runs that inning, and it looked like the ball game, especially after we scored three more in the next two frames.

The Yanks were fighting every inch of the way, though, and we went into the eighth inning only two runs ahead, 9 to 7.

Tommy Henrich opened this crucial inning for the Yanks with a base on balls from Hugh Casey. Johnny Lindell singled and Henrich stopped at second. Joe Di-Maggio, the great Yankee slugger, approached the plate. We held a conference in the infield. We had been playing a DiMag shift each time Joe had batted before, with Stanky on the shortstop side of second base, and with myself the only fielder between first and second. We decided that this time DiMag would bunt, and we didn't shift.

The Yankee Clipper didn't bunt. He took a full swing but luckily for us topped a dribbler right to Stankey. Eddie scooped up the ball, tagged Lindell on the base path, and threw to me for a double play. Henrich scored later, but that didn't matter. We won 9 to 8.

No one who saw the fourth game will ever forget it. It was the most exciting finish to any game I ever played in. Winning a game with just one hit! All day long we had been fooled by Floyd Bevens' pitches and couldn't even scratch a hit although we obtained a total of 10 walks. Then in the ninth inning, Cookie Lavagetto came up as a pinch hitter, with two out, and two walked men on base, and the score 2 to 1 in favor of the Yanks.

Cookie caught hold of one and banged it off the right field wall for a double. Our two runners scored, and as quick as you could say Jack Robinson, we had won the ball game, 3 to 2, and had tied up the Series at 2-all. All the Dodgers and almost the entire crowd at Ebbets Field came racing down on the field for Cookie. We practically ruined him, slapping his back and carrying him around the field.

I was happy that Cookie was the hero. He hadn't played much during the regular season, except as a pinch hitter. And I don't believe he had ever played first base until the time he helped me out of a spot. It was during a series at the Polo Grounds. I came up with a lame back one afternoon, and the Dodgers had no one with experience to fill in for me. I was sure if I tried to play, it would give the Giants too much of a break. Cookie took over at first during infield practice, and when game time rolled around, there he was on the bag. He played a fine game that day, and the next, too; and we kept rolling on our way to the pennant.

Well, as one fan said, "You couldn't hope to see anything again like that fourth game." Still there was the usual full house at Ebbets Field for the fifth. It was Sunday, and the last game to be played in Brooklyn. It was a game we would have liked to win.

In the third inning, Joe DiMaggio smashed a sharp grounder down to PeeWee Reese. In a twinkling of an eye, Stanky had the ball on the way to me to complete a double killing. It was the fastest play we made all year.

I was proud to be able to bring in a Dodger run. Frank Shea had already walked two, when I came up to bat. Shea is a tough pitcher to hit, but I managed to catch one squarely. This single brought in the only run we got, and the Yanks eked out a 2 to 1 victory to lead in games 3 to 2.

We had to win that sixth game, and we galloped off to a rapid start. Stanky rammed a single into left to start the first inning, and Reese followed with another single to center. I sent a towering fly into left field, very close to the foul line. Johnny Lindell lost the ball in the sun and I was safe at first. Both Stanky and Reese advanced.

Pete Reiser grounded to Stirnweiss, who tossed to Rizzuto at second. I came running down to second as tall as I could, trying to get in Rizzuto's line of vision, and I hit the bag hard in an attempt to break up the double play. Rizzuto took a tumble over my shoulder, but he made a perfect throw to first.

In the third inning, we ran the score up to 4 to 0. Reese doubled off Allie Reynolds, and I followed with another double. Dixie Walker then made it three successive doubles to score me, and to send Reynolds to the showers. We went on from there to win the game, 8 to 6, and tie up the Series again, with only one game left to play.

The final game was all in favor of the Yanks. We did come close to winning the Series, however, and we fulfilled most of the hopes that Brooklyn fans had. When Larry McPhail, president of the Yankees, said before the Series, "This is going to be tough, and I wouldn't be surprised if it went to seven games," he had hit the ball right on the nose.

In the clubhouse after the last game, Happy Chandler, Commissioner of Baseball, came in to pose for some pictures with me and Dan Bankhead, the Dodgers' Negro pitcher. He put an arm around each of us, and the photographers' bulbs flashed away.

As the Dodgers broke up to leave for their homes, we all shook hands and said good-by; and several of my teammates made me feel good by telling me that I had played a fine game of ball, all season and through the World Series, as well. And all in all, I felt it had been a good first year for me. I was happy that it had turned out that way, but I was unhappy, too, that we had not won the Series, after having battled the Yankees to the seventh game.

Burt Shotten said afterwards, "I'm sorry we didn't win it, but I have no regrets." He expressed my sentiments exactly.

After the season was over, I received a number of offers to make public appearances. The engagements were financially attractive, so I accepted. And thus ended my first year in the Big Leagues.

The active years of a Major League ball player are soon over; but while they last, they constitute the life of Riley — or so, at least, it seems to a boy who has never had much money. You stay in the best hotels (the only places I didn't stay with the team were in St. Louis and Philadelphia) . You travel on the best trains, eat the best food, and play in the best ball parks in the world. You get your name and picture in the papers. You receive invitations to all sorts of dinners and meetings. And manufacturers ask you to endorse their products. . . . Even the working conditions are good. I remember the story of a club owner who was talking salary terms with a player who was threatening to hold out. The player was pointing out that he risked his life every time he stepped up to the plate; that the earning life of a player is comparatively short, and that the money being offered him wasn't half as much as he deserved for all the chances he took while on the field.

The owner reluctantly agreed with him. "But," he said, "you can't beat the hours, Son. You can't beat the hours!"

No I don't think I could. Playing for the Brooklyn Dodgers is the best job I ever had — and I'm going to try to keep it for a long time.

That's my story. . . .

Salute

It would be absolutely impossible for me to salute all the writers across the country who supported the campaign in behalf of Negro baseball players. I would, however, like to acknowledge the efforts of Al Laney, N. Y. *Herald Tribune*; Dink Carroll, Montreal *Gazette*; Harold Atkins, Toronto *Star*; Frank Young, Chicago *Defender*; Will Connolly, San Francisco *Chronicle*; Bob Hursted, Dayton *Herald*; Dan Burley, *Amsterdam News*; Harry Keck, Pittsburgh *Sun-Telegraph*; Lem Graves, Rick Roberts, Herman Hill, Rollo Wilson, and Billy Rowe, Pittsburgh *Courier*; Roger Treat, Chicago *Herald American*; Joe Cummiskey, N. Y. *PM*; Joe Williams N. Y. *World-Telegram*; Sam Lacy, Baltimore *Afro-American*; Bill Cunningham, Boston *Herald*; Vincent X. Flaherty, Los Angeles *Examiner*; Ric Hurt, N. Y. *People's Voice*; John Carmichael, Chicago *Daily News*; Lanse McCurley, Philadelphia *Daily News*; Jack Carberry, Denver *Post*; and Lee Dunbar, Oakland *Tribune*.

I am particularly indebted to the following writers assigned to cover the Dodgers. Roscoe McGowen, N. Y. *Times*; Mike Gavan, N. Y. *Journal American*; Arch Murray, N. Y. *Post*; Harold Burr, Brooklyn *Eagle*; Gus Steiger, N. Y. *Daily Mirror*; Dick Young, N. Y. *Daily News*; Bill Roeder, N. Y. *World-Telegram*; Bob Cook, N. Y. *Herald Tribune*; and Herb Goren, N. Y. *Sun*.

And last, but far from least, I want to express my gratitude to Red Barber and Connie Desmond, the radio announcers of all Dodger games.

Acknowledgments

Pictures on pages 35, 36, 38, 39 and 40 by courtesy of the Asucla News Bureau.

Pictures on pages 42, 44, 45, 47, 48, 87, 88, 89, 90, 91, 92, 94, 95, 96, 131, 133, 139 and 142 by courtesy of International News Service.

Picture on page 41 by courtesy of *Our World* magazine.

Picture on page 43 by courtesy of United Service Organizations.

Pictures on pages 46, 82, 84, 86 and 141 by courtesy of New York *Daily News.*

Pictures on pages 93, 129, 132, 134, 136, 137 and 140 by courtesy of Press Association, Inc.

Picture on page 138 by courtesy of Wide World Photos.

Picture on page 144 by courtesy of General Artists Corp.

Pictures on pages 81, 83, 85, 130, 135 and 143 by courtesy of Chick Solomon and the *Amsterdam News.*

CPSIA information can be obtained
at www.ICGtesting.com
Printed in the USA
BVHW080901070121
597128BV00003B/163

9 781626 549401